BRING

HOME

the JOY

BRING

HOME

the JOY

larry CRABB   dr. kevin LEMAN
les & leslie PARROTT   gary SMALLEY
becky and roger TIRABASSI
and neil clark WARREN

ZondervanPublishingHouse
Grand Rapids, Michigan

A Division of HarperCollins*Publishers*

Bring Home the Joy
Copyright © 1998 by Women of Faith, Inc.

Requests for information should be addressed to:

 Zondervan Publishing House
Grand Rapids, Michigan 49530

Library of Congress Cataloging-in-Publication Data

Bring home the joy : best-selling authors share the secrets of adding enjoyment and vitality to
    your marriage / Larry Crabb ... [et al.].
        p.   cm.
    Excerpts reprinted from the authors' books.
    Includes bibliographical references.
    ISBN 0-310-22786-0 (hardcover)
    1. Marriage.   2. Marriage—Religious aspects—Christianity.   I. Crabb, Lawrence J.
HQ734.B8154. 1998
306.81—dc21   98-34523
                                                                              CIP

This edition is printed on acid-free paper and meets the American National Standards Institute
Z39.48 standard.

All Scripture quotations, unless otherwise indicated, are taken from *The Holy Bible, New
International Version®*. NIV®. Copyright© 1973, 1984 by International Bible Society. Used by
permission of Zondervan Publishing House. All rights reserved.

Scripture references marked NASB are taken from the *New American Standard Bible* (NASB), ©
1960, 1977 by the Lockman Foundation.

Portions of this book are taken from:

Larry Crabb, *Men & Women: Enjoying the Difference* (Grand Rapids: Zondervan, 1991, 1993).
Used by permission.

Dr. Kevin Leman, *Keeping Your Family Together When the World Is Falling Apart* (New York:
Delacorte, 1992). Used by permission of Dr. Kevin Leman.

Les and Leslie Parrott, *Like a Kiss on the Lips* (Zondervan, 1997) and *Saving Your Marriage
Before It Starts* (Zondervan, 1995). Used by permission.

Gary Smalley, *Hidden Keys of a Loving, Lasting Marriage* (Zondervan, 1984, 1988). Used by
permission.

The Triumphant Marriage by Neil Clark Warren, Ph.D., a Focus on the Family book published
by Tyndale House. Copyright © 1995 by Neil Clark Warren, Ph.D. All rights reserved.
International copyright secured. Used by permission.

Becky and Dr. Roger Tirabassi, *How to Live with Them Since You Can't Live Without Them*
(Nashville: Thomas Nelson, 1998). Used by permission.

Printed in the United States of America

---

98 99 00 01 02 03 04 05 /❖ DC/ 10 9 8 7 6 5 4 3 2 1

CONTENTS

FOREWORD

Imagine that you and your spouse could sit down with six of the country's most experienced and sought-after marriage counselors. Think how their joyful encouragement could inspire you; ponder how their astute marital advice could transform your marriage. Picture yourselves smiling at their insights (*How did they know we do that?*) and blinking as they pinpoint your problems (*You mean we're not the only ones with that struggle?*). In *Bring Home the Joy,* you'll find yourselves having that kind of close encounter with some of America's most popular marriage experts.

I am grateful to Sue Ann Jones for compiling this book from the writings of six counselors who are known for their light-hearted humor, down-to-earth anecdotes, and rock-solid advice. As conference speakers, workshop leaders, and authors they have shared their knowledge in settings across the country. Now they join together to *Bring Home the Joy,* offering you the best of their enthusiasm and sharply focused advice in one informative and spirit-lifting book. Within these pages you will find discussed the issues that confront and confound many married couples today—issues like love, forgiveness, sex, spirituality, self-centeredness, work, and boredom.

And these are no dry, pedantic lectures. The advice shared here is offered with a twinkling eye and a merry soul, because these counselors are not just marriage experts. They are happily married spouses themselves. They don't just share their knowledge as counselors but also their own years of marriage, the good times and the bad, and how they've laughed about, cried over, and learned from their own experiences.

Each chapter looks at a different component of a joyful marriage with refreshing candor and appealing anecdotes. But again and again in these pages you will find strands of the same common cord of solid wisdom—principles on how to keep God foremost in your relationship, how to love your partner as yourself, how to keep the spark of new love alive, how to nurture each other, forgive each other, talk to each other, praise and support each other—even how to fight a good fight with each other!

Whether you've been married for decades or only for days, I hope you and your mate will read this book together. May you gain from it the inspiration and motivation to make your marriage better—and then to *Bring Home the Joy.*

—Stephen Arterburn

Introduction

RIGHT HERE, RIGHT NOW*

Dr. Les Parrott

For six years of graduate school I had a small sign pinned on a corkboard above the desk where I spent most of my time. It was a quote from Abraham Maslow: "Some people spend their entire lives indefinitely preparing to live."

Hardly a week went by that I did not ponder that statement and desperately try not to focus all of my energy on the future. I needed that little reminder because I often felt as though my life was on hold—like someone had pushed the pause button—until I completed my degree. *After graduation,* I would tell myself, *we'll move into a bigger apartment . . . we'll take a long vacation . . . I'll have a real job with normal hours . . . I'll eat better . . . we'll go out on more dates . . .*

After graduation, however, it wasn't long before I found myself saying, *Once I get tenure as a professor . . . Once I finish writing this book . . . Once we own our own house . . .* and on and on.

It's tempting to boast about tomorrow. After all, the future holds many exciting possibilities. But when we focus our attention on what is around the corner, we miss out on what we have right now. And that is particularly true in marriage.

We often plan the perfect romantic evening in a candlelit restaurant, for example, and miss out on the loving moment in the glare of sunshine on our own doorstep. That's inspired marriage experts to label the greetings and good-byes we have with our mates as the most important moments of the day.

---

*Taken from *Like a Kiss on the Lips* by Les and Leslie Parrott. Copyright © 1997 by Les and Leslie Parrott. Used by permission.

When a husband and wife come together after an absence—upon waking, getting home from work, or returning from a trip—the first few minutes will set the stage for how the rest of the time will go. Family therapist Marcia Lasswell says, "It's very important that the first few minutes of reconnection be positive and supportive. We all know how good it feels to walk into someone's presence and have them look up and smile, and how awful it is if he or she is preoccupied or negative." We know this because the "It's-good-to-see-you" look is what we instinctively gave, and received, in the early stages of our dating relationship.

So boast about tomorrow if you must, dream big dreams about your future, but don't forsake right here and right now. Your marriage will thank you.

Chapter One

A SUCCESSFUL MARRIAGE:
IT'S EASIER THAN YOU THINK*

Gary Smalley

When I was newly married, I often asked other couples if they could tell me the secrets of a happy marriage. They would usually say, "You and your wife will have problems, but if it's meant to be, you'll stay together; if not, you'll separate." Later, when I worried about staying close to my children, people would answer, "Your teenagers will rebel. It's just normal."

These philosophies seemed so pessimistic that I became discouraged whenever our domestic harmony was threatened during an argument. I couldn't find any articles or books written on how to become a warm, loving family.

However, today I can say without reservation that my wife is my best friend. This has come about because we have practiced a principle learned from several successful families. Practicing this principle also has eliminated any significant disharmony in our family and has drawn us all closer.

I learned this principle by interviewing over a hundred couples across the nation. I chose them initially because they seemed to have close relationships with their children. Though many were teenagers, all seemed to be close to their parents and happy about it. They were enthusiastic families, radiantly happy in most instances.

When I spoke to different groups, I would scan the audience, looking for the family that seemed the happiest. Then I would

---

*Adapted from *The Hidden Keys of a Loving, Lasting Marriage* by Gary Smalley. Copyright © 1984, 1988 by Gary Smalley. Used by permission.

interview them afterward. I often talked to the wife alone, then the husband, and finally the children. I always asked them the same questions: "What do you believe is the main reason you're all so close and happy as a family?" Without exception, each member of each family gave the same answer: "We do a lot of things together." Even more amazing to me was that all the families had one particular activity in common.

I can truthfully say I have tested the suggestions of these families enough to prove they are valid. I no longer fear my family will break up. Nor do I fear my children will reject my wife and me as they grow older. That's because my family is practicing the things those other successful families suggested.

SHARE EXPERIENCES TOGETHER

Jesus left us an example by sharing his life with the disciples. They traveled, ate, slept, healed, and ministered together. He guided, guarded, and kept them; then he prayed for them (see John 17). His example of togetherness and oneness constantly inspires me to become "one" with my family by scheduling many times to be together.

Since every family I interviewed specifically mentioned camping, I looked into it as a possible recreational activity. Norma's first thought was of bugs, snakes, dirt, and all sorts of creepy-crawlys. She didn't like camping. Though I had been camping only a few times, I couldn't remember having any insurmountable problems. We decided to give it a try. Norma reluctantly agreed, frantically clutching a can of insect repellent and stuffing mosquito coils into her purse.

We borrowed a pop-up camper and headed for Florida. We found a beautiful campsite in Kentucky, and though I was nervous being all alone in the woods, I didn't say anything. After we parked next to the only bright streetlight within fifty feet of the showers, we built a campfire to roast hot dogs and marshmallows. It was peaceful. No one was around to distract us. We put the children to bed around nine, and then Norma and I stayed up to enjoy a romantic evening. A distant thunderstorm entertained us with a light show as we enjoyed a warm breeze. Though the lightning came closer and closer, we thought it was passing to one side of us and went to bed with light hearts.

The children were asleep as I crawled into a tiny bed with Greg, and Norma joined Kari. We were lying close enough to touch hands while we whispered softly. I thought, *Boy, this is really the life. I can see why everybody likes to camp.* But my feeling of serenity was blasted away as the storm began to lash furiously around us and knocked out the streetlight beside our tent. It was pitch black except for the frequent jagged streaks illuminating the sky. Thunder rumbled, shaking the ground beneath us, and the wind began to howl. Rain beat against our tent until the water forced its way through, soaking our pillows.

"Honey, do you think this camper is going to blow over?" Norma asked faintly.

"No, not a chance," I said. I really thought the camper was going to blow *up*. I knew we were going to die. But within an hour, the storm's wrath cooled enough to let the stars shine through again. We lay there breathlessly on our soaked pillows, each wondering silently whether camping was the life for us. I was also curious as to why camping played such an important part in drawing families together. Of course, any family that faced sure death together and survived would be closer!

Colorado was the destination for our own trip in our own trailer. We could hardly wait to experience the beauty of snow-capped peaks and sniff the aroma of pine trees. I could already hear the sizzle of rainbow trout frying in the pan. As we started up the mountain, our station wagon slowed from fifty miles per hour to thirty, then to twenty-five, then to twenty, until we finally slowed to the pace of fifteen miles per hour. "Hot" read the temperature gauge. I felt like I was wired to the engine because my palms were sweating so. Our children sensed the tension in the air and became hyper and loud.

"I've got to stop at the next pull-off area," I told them. My nerves were frayed as I pulled over. All three kids jumped out immediately. I hadn't even had time to worry about the overheated car when our youngest, Michael, screamed at the top of his lungs.

His older brother, relieving some pent-up energy, had kicked what he thought to be an empty can. Unfortunately, it was half-full of transmission fluid. The can had landed upside down on Michael's head, and he was covered from head to toe, a terribly unhappy little boy. His nose, his ears, even his mouth were dripping with it. Not expecting such a calamity, we had no water in the trailer with which to clean him up. We worried that he had injured his eyes because he blinked rapidly the rest of the trip.

I've mentioned only the tragic times of our camping experiences, but we've also had tremendous experiences hiking to tops of mountains and exploring the out-of-doors. But the real significance of camping will be understood, I believe, when we get to the third point discussed in this chapter.

Doing things with your family may cost you a little extra money, but it's worth every penny.

For example, Norma called one day to ask if I would like to buy a water-skiing boat and equipment. Though I was unsure at first, the idea seemed to appeal to everyone in the family. We purchased an "extremely experienced" model. When we were bouncing across the lake on our first time out, I noticed my wife holding on to the side as if she feared we would capsize at any moment. I thought I had everything under control, yet panic was clearly written on her face.

She gripped the windshield with one hand while the other had a death grip on the bar beside her.

"Norma, what's wrong?" I questioned.

"I hate boats," she said slowly.

"You've got to be kidding! You hate boats? You're the one who called me up and said you wanted to buy the boat, and now you're telling me you hate boats? Would you like to explain that?"

I slowed our speed and let the boat idle so she could relax enough to talk to me.

"All my life I've been afraid of boats," she said. "I've just always had a real problem with boats." I sat there in total bewilderment.

She labored to explain that she hated boats, but she knew she could learn to like them. She enjoys them much more now, further convinced that boating and skiing will knit our lives together. She determined to endure boating long enough to learn to like it for the family's sake.

Not long after our first boating experience, I sat next to an executive from Boeing Aircraft on a flight to Seattle. When I asked him about his family, he told me they were very close.

"What is the most important thing that holds your family together?" I asked.

"Several years ago," he said, "we purchased a yacht, and as a family we traveled around the various inlets and islands in the Seattle area. My family enjoys boating so much that it has provided a tremendous way to knit us together."

I wish all fathers felt that way.

One man sadly admitted that when he and his children meet for a rare get-together, they hardly have a thing in common.

"It's a sickening experience," he said, "to have your children back home for a visit and have nothing in common. You know, the only thing we ever laugh about as a family is when we remember the one time we took a three-week vacation. We rented a tent and camped. What a vacation! We still laugh at those experiences."

He didn't have any other fond memories of family togetherness.

His wife had her women's clubs; he had his men's clubs; the children had their activities. They all grew apart in separate worlds.

"Now that my wife and I are alone, we have very little in common," he lamented. "We are two lonely people lost in our five-bedroom house."

The simple principle of sharing life together has permeated every area of our family life, from supporting Greg and Michael in soccer to supporting Kari and Greg in piano. As much as possible, we look for ways to spend time together—cooking, fishing, putting the kids to bed, gardening. Everything we do as a family assures me of our unity later in life.

When I think of a trip to Hawaii, I envision snorkeling, scuba diving, spearfishing, or anything related to being in the water. My wife thinks of an orchid lei as she steps off the airplane, dining in romantic restaurants, renting a car, and sight-seeing during the day. Our desires are completely different. We feel that although a husband and wife both need time to enjoy separate activities, they also need to step into the world of their mates to taste each other's interests.

While my wife is shopping, I might be snorkeling, but at night we would dine together in a very romantic place. At times my wife would want to snorkel with me, and I would enjoy sight-seeing with her. I'm not saying that I would rather be touring than snorkeling or that she would rather slip on a wet suit instead of a new dress, but we believe it is important to compromise in order to share experiences. Afterward, when the trip is only a motel receipt in your wallet, it's experiences you shared during the trip that will draw you together.

I often ask couples if they ever do things together. When I ask about vacations and the husband's face lights up while the wife grimaces, I usually conclude they took their vacation at the husband's chosen site. It was probably a dream to him and sheer torture for her and the children.

Consider the following suggestions before planning a family outing.

First, find out what activities you and your wife and your children would like to do together. Next, consider everyone's schedule to see if the planned outing will force hardship on anyone involved. For example, we agreed as a family that Greg should not be involved in group sports until this season because we felt we should be camping on weekends instead of sitting on bleachers watching one member play football. From time to time, we adjust our schedule to make sure our family activities are not forcing one member to miss an important event.

At this point, ask your wife to name ten activities she would enjoy doing with you throughout the year.

Next, ask her to rate which activity of the ten is the most important to her. Don't be surprised if she prefers doing some things alone—or if she doesn't enjoy being with you at all. If she has no desire to share activities with you, reflect on your attitude toward her in the past. Have you been critical or bored? Did you pout when you had to do something she wanted to do? If so, she will remember those times and tend to avoid involvement with you in the future.

Now, let's go on to the second suggestion for becoming a close-knit family.

RECOGNIZE EVERYONE'S NEED TO BELONG

You and I know the good feeling we have when we're able to say, "I belong to this club"; "these are my friends"; "the club needs my help."

During an interview with a pro-football cheerleader, I learned how much wives need to feel that sense of belonging. She told me she loved the way her husband treated her when she returned from a two-day trip. He was so excited to have her home. He pampered her, telling her how much he had missed her. But his appreciative attitude usually wore off in about two days. Then he would start taking her for granted again.

Men, why do we sit glued to the television as though our wives didn't exist? It seems we realize our love for them most when they're out of our lives for a few days. But after we've had them with us for a while, the "ho-hums" set in, don't they?

The principle of belonging is powerfully illustrated by an experience I had with my daughter. When Kari was nine years old, I sensed an undefined barrier between us. I couldn't detect anything specific. We just weren't close. I didn't enjoy being with her, and she didn't enjoy me either. No matter how hard I tried, I couldn't break through the barrier. From time to time, Norma would comment that I preferred my sons over my daughter. I said, "One of the reasons is because the boys are more responsive to me."

"You'd better do something to strengthen the relationship now," Norma said, "because when Kari gets older it will be much harder." So I tested the value of belonging and decided to take Kari with me on my next seven-day business trip. Though we still weren't close, she became excited as we planned what to do and where to stay. During the plane trip we worked on her multiplication problems until it almost drove me crazy—and the man in front of us. We stayed with a farm family in Washington the first night. I noticed the rapport Kari and I felt as we laughed and sang around the dinner table with their numerous children; we were actually enjoying one another's company. At times we didn't even talk. It seemed enough just to be together. Kari seemed to have just as much fun in that farm home as she did helping me with my meetings. I let her distribute some of the material so she really felt she was a special part of my team. And she was.

We decided to take the scenic route from Portland to Seattle. I wanted to show her the small "poke and plum" town near Portland where I was raised. (It's so small that by the time you "poke" your head out of the window you're "plum" out of the town.) After we had a flat tire near the Columbia River, we changed it together and then walked down to the river to gather driftwood for a memento. We tried to make it up a snow-covered mountain but had to turn around and go all the way back to Seattle the long way. We will both remember that trip, good times and bad.

I have never sensed a barrier between us in the years since that trip. I feel complete harmony and oneness in Kari's company. She still has the piece of driftwood sitting in her bedroom, a silent reminder of our bond and her special relationship with Christ; on it is engraved her salvation date.

LET HARD TIMES DRAW YOU TOGETHER

Foxholes make lasting friendships. Haven't you heard the stories of buddies who shared the same foxhole during wartime? Whenever they meet, there is an instant camaraderie that no one can ever take away from them, a feeling born from surviving a struggle together. Trials can produce maturity and loving attitudes (see James 1:2–4).

Families have foxholes too. Even when a crisis inflicts deep scars, the dilemma can draw the family closer.

Maybe it's the crises in camping that have such a unifying effect on a family. Any family that can survive bugs, poison ivy, storms, burnt sausage, and sand in the eggs has to come out of the ordeal closer. During a crisis, you have only each other to rely on. We all look back on the mishaps that occurred during our camping trips and *laugh,* though it wasn't a bit funny at the time. Like the night Norma awakened me at two in the morning so cold that she asked, "Honey, could you take us home?" Though we were two hours from home, I abandoned my cozy bed to pack and leave. She called me her John Wayne on the way home, but at the time I didn't feel much like the Duke.

Our camping fiascoes have been numerous. *Only two more hours and home sweet home,* I thought after our first camping trip. Tension electrified the air as we all longed to be home with hot water and familiar beds once again. Now when we look back on the experience we laugh, and our laughter binds us together as husband and wife and as parents and children.

THE ONE ACTIVITY THAT WIVES ENJOY MOST WITH THEIR HUSBANDS

Many women have told me about the importance of intimate communication with their husbands—special togetherness times—after the children are in bed, during the day on the telephone, at breakfast, at dinner, at a restaurant over a cup of coffee. These special sharing times can be the most enjoyable part of a woman's day.

My wife agrees that an intimate sharing time with me is the one thing she enjoys most about our relationship. We make it a point to have breakfast together as often as possible at a nearby restaurant just to talk about our upcoming schedules. I ask her questions about what she needs for the week and what I can do to help her and vice versa. I enjoy our discussions because I know she enjoys them. But more importantly, I would really miss those times of intimate communication if we ever neglected them.

To really understand each other during our conversations, we use a concept called the "revolving method" of communication. Though it's very simple, you'll find it a tremendous help in avoiding misunderstandings. It involves four steps:

1. I ask my wife to share her feelings or thoughts with me.
2. I respond by rephrasing what I think she said.
3. She answers either yes or no.
4. If she answers no, I continue to rephrase what I think she said until I get a yes response.

My wife goes through the same four steps when I am explaining my feelings to her.

Our communication is more meaningful since neither of us assumes we automatically know what the other is saying. (In the past, misunderstandings over implied meanings confused and ruined many discussions.) This process has nearly eliminated misinterpretations in our marriage.

Chapter Two

GET TOUGH!*

Dr. Neil Clark Warren

Does one of the following describe marriage for you?

- You fell in love, the question was "popped," the wedding was a wonderful success, and marriage is now a continual joyride for both of you.
- You fell in love, the wedding was a mixture of stress and success, and marriage is a wagon-train trip across the plains and over the mountains to the old west.
- You fell in love, the wedding was a series of problems to be solved, and marriage is a marathon run on a hot, summer day through hill country.
- You fell in love, the wedding was an expensive headache, and marriage is a bloody gunfight at the OK Corral.

Which of these scenarios would characterize your marriage? Has it been a joyride or a gunfight—or something in between? The majority of married people I know, especially the ones who are still alive and married, talk about their experience as "somewhere in between," not exactly a joyride all the time, but not a gunfight either.

I'm fully aware that a few married people describe their relationships as "nothing but wonderful" or "a sleigh ride on a snowy night with the bells on the horses jingling and the sound of a

---

*Adapted from *The Triumphant Marriage* by Neil Clark Warren, Ph.D. a Focus on the Family book published by Tyndale House. Copyright © 1995 by Neil Clark Warren, Ph.D. All rights reserved. International copyright secured. Used by permission.

carol-singing choir in the background." Some people believe that marriage can be a perpetual joyride. That may be true for some, but not for most people.

For most people, the demands of marriage are mind-boggling. It requires all the energy you can give it—and then it asks for more. It involves a continual need for negotiation and compromise, for give and more give.

Mind you, I'm a big believer in marriage. I have never seen happier, more deeply satisfied people than men and women who have made their marriages work. But neither have I met many people in highly successful marriages who got there without an enormous expenditure of energy and determination. There were times when they simply had to be "willful." Virtually every successful marriage requires all kinds of willpower. Sometimes issues arise and the partners don't have the necessary skills to manage them. They essentially have two choices: give up and run away, or get about the task of developing the required skills. Partners with willpower always adopt the second alternative. They wouldn't think of giving up. They are ready to go to work on the problem, ready to do whatever they must to keep their marriage healthy for a lifetime.

The foundation of willpower is a set of marital promises. It is this set of promises that serves as the steel structure of every great marriage. Both partners need to know exactly what they originally promised to each other, and they need to be *currently* committed to those promises so that their willpower will always be stronger than *any* opposing force.

Marriage doesn't just happen! It takes a solid set of decisions, a huge amount of skill, and enormous willpower. I contend that people in extremely healthy marriages *built* those marriages just as you build a mammoth bridge or a skyscraper. They made their marriage triumphant because they simply wouldn't settle for less. It doesn't matter at all to them how much backbreaking work it requires; if it were necessary, they would do a thousand times more. Their willpower gives them this kind of toughness.

COMMITMENT: THE CORNERSTONE
OF A TRIUMPHANT MARRIAGE

Marriage is so difficult and requires so much toughness that, as a society, we ask persons entering marriage to take some hard-hitting, heavy-duty vows. We know how easy it will be for them to give up along the way, to claim that they didn't know marriage could be so demanding. We gather into small or large groups just to hear them take these vows, and the people who are already married know that there are going to be times when these newlyweds will have to refer back to their vows—with the future of their marriage hanging in the balance.

Unfortunately, these vows are often treated with incredible superficiality. Maybe that's because society has only recently recognized the deadly serious dilemma we're in when it comes to marital instability. With a divorce rate that has us reeling, our nation is waking up fast to how fiercely difficult it is to make a marriage work. We are beginning to recognize how grossly we have underestimated the difficulty of marriage and how under-equipped marital participants have been. As a nation, we have reached the edge of total family collapse.

When I read the inventories of the 200 spouses in our advisory group—100 couples in extremely healthy marriages—I was overwhelmed at the frequency with which they emphasized the critical importance of commitment. One man said it succinctly: "Our lives are the sum total of our commitments. Commitment is the essence of what marriage is all about." More than 90 percent of the respondents echoed his words. Everywhere I turned in these inventories, I heard the same powerful opinion: "Marriage demands toughness, and toughness proceeds out of commitment.

No marriage will ever be stronger than the commitment that serves as its infrastructure."

Jeanette and Robert Lauer published the results of their powerful study a few years ago.[1] They surveyed 351 couples who had been married 15 or more years. Of the 351 couples, 300 said they were happily married. Each husband and wife responded individually to a questionnaire that included thirty-nine statements and questions about marriage. They were asked to select from their answers "the ones that best-explained why their marriages had lasted." Out of thirty-nine important reasons, two of the four rated "most important" for both men and women were "Marriage is a long-term commitment" and "Marriage is sacred."

Yale professor Robert Sternberg has frequently cited commitment as crucial to a successful marriage. Here are his words:

> Loving relationships almost inevitably have their ups and downs, and there may be times in such relationships when the decision/commitment component is all or almost all that keeps the relationship going. This component can be essential for getting through hard times and returning to better ones. In ignoring it or separating it from love, one may be missing exactly that component of loving relationships that enables one to get through the hard times as well as the easy ones.[2]

It is a tough-sounding vow that society asks people entering marriage to take, and it should be. If they are to be successful, they must be prepared for a major contest. They need to be trained and toughened—and why not? We require our citizens to prepare long and hard for careers. We put soldiers, police officers, and firefighters through rigorous training programs. We expect athletes and athletic teams to practice for months so they will be equal to the challenge of competition. But we are in the habit of sending persons into marriage with virtually no understanding of the challenges they will face. The inevitable massacre is tragically predictable! The bottom line is that marriage is often tougher than marital participants are. That can change.

SKILLS NECESSARY FOR A TRIUMPHANT MARRIAGE

We must understand that commitment alone is only part of the equation for a triumphant marriage. Commitment must lead to skill development. I have never studied a great marriage in which I viewed the partners as anything less than profoundly skillful. It's crucial to recognize, though, that much of the time, these skills were learned and developed *after* the marriage began. Often, the development of the skills came in response to a crisis or a series of crises.

Many persons in our group of 100 healthy marriages encountered enormous problems in their marriages, and in response to those problems, they learned marriage-saving skills. If those skills were learned unusually well, the crisis was not only handled, but the marriage also took on a new level of strength and satisfaction that would not have been available if the crisis had not emerged. Marriage-saving skills became vital resources in building a great relationship.

THE MATTER OF WILLPOWER

Well in advance of skill development, though, is the matter of willpower. Hundreds of thousands of marriages fall apart before the necessary skills can be developed because there is inadequate willpower. If a marriage relies forever on willpower, it will eventually become worn out and emaciated. Nevertheless, a marriage short on willpower is vulnerable to extinction when the road gets rocky and the challenges mount.

Willpower and commitment are closely related. Persons tend to have a greater desire to do those things that they have promised to do. If they promised to cherish the other person under every kind of circumstance for as long as they live, and if this promise is current and vital, the likelihood that their spouse will be cherished in a difficult moment is substantially higher.

If I am deeply aware of a particular promise I have made to you, I will try hard to keep it. For instance, if I promise to love you even when we have lost all our money, I will try to love you under the worst of economic conditions. If I find it difficult to love you under those circumstances, I will look for help in learning how to—because I am acutely aware that I *promised* to love you. Promises strengthen my level of willfulness. When I promise to do something, it maximizes the strength of my determination, and I pump up my willpower to its highest level.

If I lack the skill to do what I promised to do, my high level of willpower will make me persevere. And this same willpower will make me search to find resources to increase my skill level. I *will* myself to love you, and I *will* it so much that I will do anything to learn how to make it happen.

YOUR CURRENT LEVEL OF COMMITMENT

One of the chief determinants of marital willpower's strength is the degree to which your promises to your spouse are current—that is, the degree to which you passionately affirm them *today*.

Marriage counselors and psychologists observe that most married persons' awareness of the promises they made at their wedding declines over time. Moreover, the promises they do remember seem less vital and less passionately held as time passes.

The fact is that most persons who enter marriage take their vows in a haphazard, superficial way. They stand in front of a minister, priest, rabbi, or justice of the peace, and they are asked to repeat some words ... which they do with considerable nervousness. If you asked them a half-hour after the wedding to tell you what they had promised, most of them would have only a fuzzy recollection.

That's part of the reason most "older-married people" in our society have little more than a superficial understanding of what they pledged to their mate. I have asked scores of these persons what marital commitment is all about, and they nearly always respond with some form of "stick it out." Of course, that's the *least* important part of the pledge they took. A marriage in which two people are in deep emotional pain but simply stick it out because they promised to is a marriage that will be in deep emotional pain forever.

Sticking it out is worth virtually nothing in a marital crisis, except it gives you an additional chance to make it better. But if all you do the next time is stick it out, your whole marriage will be a series of "sticking it out" experiences, which usually results in a horribly sick marriage. There's no real growth or improvement; it's a matter of muddling through one crisis after another.

THE ESSENCE OF COMMITMENT

Commitment requires a far more active approach in marriage, and certainly during a time of marital challenge. Staying in a marriage can be totally passive; you don't leave, but you don't do anything to make the marriage better.

The radical part of the commitment vow is that you promise to *love* the other person through every kind of circumstance for as long as you both live. Moreover, you promise to *honor* and *cherish* your mate. Not only that, but you also promise to perform every duty that a husband or wife owes to his or her spouse as long as you both live. So there are four huge promises that you make to your spouse—all of which are highly active, all of which involve only *your* action, all of which you make unilaterally and unequivocally for as long as you live—no matter what!

Active commitment means that if you are tempted to pick up and run, you yourself block both exits. "I'll tell you what," you say to your spouse, "I'll make you these promises for as long as we both are alive, *and* there is no condition to my promises. If things get really bad, you can depend on me. Furthermore, I will never go out and find a substitute mate."

If married people kept their promises, not only would the divorce rate be obliterated, but marriages would also get significantly better! Show me a marriage in which even one person keeps this pledge with passion, and I'll show you a marriage with a lot of value. Show me a relationship in which both persons keep this pledge, and I'll show you a relationship headed for greatness.

It goes without saying that commitment has become an incredibly cheap concept in our culture. Most married people don't have the foggiest notion of what they have committed themselves to. But worst of all, there is little about the "promises" of marriage that is *current* for most married people. Like one middle-aged man said to me while in the heat of a major marital crisis, "Listen, I took those vows a long time ago, and that's all ancient history."

So what's the solution to this dilemma? First, we have to develop something like "informed consent" when it comes to marriage. We simply must not let any new marriages begin unless the two people really know what they are promising each other. Second, we need to encourage people who are already married to recommit themselves to each other—but only after they have carefully understood *exactly* what the marital promises are all about.

MARITAL TOUGHNESS REQUIRES CONTINUAL FITNESS

The problems for a marriage in this society are too demanding for out-of-shape marital players to handle. There are so many ways that a marriage can be destroyed; in order for it to be successful, both marriage partners must be highly focused and highly energized. This focus and energy come directly from a keen sense of the promises they have made. These promises must be as current as their breathing.

If these promises have not been burned into their brains, the inevitable problems will roll right over the top of them. Their marriage will be demolished. My experience tells me that a high proportion of married people are totally unfit to face complex marital challenges. Often, they have become flabby from inattention to their original decision—their early commitment. They have done almost nothing *recently* to prepare themselves for the demanding events that are always lurking. They are like tennis players who haven't played for a long time. When they face an opponent who is well practiced and in peak condition, they get slaughtered. They aren't ready! How come? Because no one warned them to stay tough! Why not? Because everyone, especially the two of them, simply assumed that they could make it fine on the basis of their love, warm feelings, and past successes. This assumption is absurd, but it is responsible for the overpowering of out-of-shape marriage partners by the enormously demanding, but inevitable, problems involved in building a successful marriage.

I am convinced that until we start seeing marriage more realistically, the divorce rate is going to stay at epidemic levels. Marriage is incredibly difficult! We had better start recognizing this. Anyone who is going to succeed in marriage needs determination. Obviously, great skillfulness is required, but the development of the necessary skills often takes time. That's why you need to have a current, deeply owned, thoroughly rehearsed set of promises to your mate. If you don't have this, if you're out of shape, if you aren't ready for a slew of tough battles that will test your strength and your endurance, then you are in danger of becoming a divorce statistic.

BOOT CAMP FOR COMMITMENT TRAINING

I take couples into training, preferably before they are disillusioned about how impossible marriage is. If they are reasonably well matched as partners, I am convinced that I can prepare them for the inevitable challenges—and virtually assure them of victory nearly every time they experience a struggle.

How do I do this? Here are the three fundamental sections of the training course.

Section #1: Getting Clear About What to Expect

One of the major causes of marital deterioration is unrealistic expectations of those entering marriage. Nearly one-half of all divorces occur within two years of the wedding day. This is a clear indication that people are shocked about what they find marriage to be like.

I try to help those who are entering marriage to expect a relational situation requiring all kinds of change and growth. One analogy I use involves golf. When you pay your green fee, you are admitted to the course. As you stand on the first tee, you are faced with the challenge to hit the ball straight if you are to avoid the trees on the left and the water on the right. But if there were no sand traps, no trees, no water, and no out of bounds, there would be little reason for you to play. Similarly, when you marry, you stand on the first tee, so to speak, and await the action. The very thrill of marriage involves meeting the challenges and improving your game. But the point is that when you get married, the obstacles and the dangers are still out in front of you.

The principal challenge of marriage is the weaving together of two complex individual identities and the forming of a corporate identity. The building of a corporate identity, or oneness, is particularly attractive because it offers the potential to meet basic, individual needs in a far more deeply satisfying way than they have ever been met before. But the formation of the corporate identity requires significant flexibility and elasticity on the part of both individuals. Continual negotiation and compromise are essential. If the individual identities are too fragile or too rigid, all of this adaptation will exact too great a price, create too much anxiety, and cause excessive pain. The challenge of building a corporate identity—which requires each partner to make contributions and modifications—is what makes marriage so attractive but so incredibly difficult.

This is exactly where marital toughness comes in. There is plenty of temptation to run, to just consider the whole matter too complex or impossible. But if you're tough, you keep moving ahead. You seek the counsel you need. You stay focused. You don't stop until you're victorious.

These marital problems have a way of staying after you forever. How long two people have been married has some impact on the number of marital challenges they will face, since many issues are worked out over time. But don't fool yourself: As long as two individuals are involved, there will always be issues to be addressed. My wife and I have been married for thirty-six years, and we deal with new or unresolved issues virtually every month. Although we have worked through thousands of issues over the years, our individuality still poses problems for our corporate identity.

The strongest message married people need to hear is that they should expect a significant number of hassles, demands for change, power struggles, and hard-to-deal-with conflicts. The more complex their individual identities, the greater the challenges are likely to be. But at the same time, the more differentiated they are as persons, the greater their potential for weaving together a corporate identity that will be rich with variation, breadth, and satisfaction.

Section #2: Developing a Thorough and Insightful Understanding of the Marital Promises

I have already mentioned that the vast majority of married persons have almost no understanding of what they have promised to their mate. It isn't that their memory is faulty; they simply didn't have a firm grasp of what their vows meant when they originally said them. Making a marriage work, especially during times of severe marital challenge, requires a "promise orientation" that is highly enlightened.

If you analyze the traditional marriage vows, you will discover six separate parts:

1. I will love you as long as we both live.
2. I will cherish you as long as we both live.
3. I will honor you as long as we both live.
4. I will be for you everything that a husband or wife owes to their spouse.
5. I will never give my love to, or get romantically involved with, another person.
6. I will do all five of these things under every kind of condition for as long as we live.

Put another way, I promise to love, honor, and cherish you—and to be entirely responsible in relation to you under *every* kind of circumstance for as long as we live.

The marriage vow says that if my wife and I don't agree about something, I promise to take her position seriously and to honor her, even in the midst of our disagreement. If I don't get what I think I need from her, I promise not to withhold anything I owe to her, and furthermore, I promise to remain loyal to her. My promises do not mean that I will ignore our differences or fail to stand up for my own thoughts, feelings, and rights, but they do mean that I will never stop loving her and cherishing her, no matter what.

Section #3: Rehearsing the Marital Promises Until They Are Burned into the Brain

The marriage vows are typically spoken during a single occasion under high-anxiety circumstances. Because of this, they frequently have little value in the midst of a marital crisis. Most often, they are about as influential on behavior as a New Year's resolution—nothing more than an idealized wish. New Year's resolutions are usually broken early in the year, often before New Year's Day has been fully celebrated. Moreover, marriage vows seldom have anything like an effective operational plan connected with them.

A few days or a few months after the vows are taken, whatever minimal power they had to influence behavior earlier is usually lost. Because the vows are not repeated over time, their current influence on attitude and behavior becomes less and less significant.

That's exactly why I am proposing to change the frequency of the marriage vow. Instead of its being taken once in a lifetime under stressful conditions, I suggest that it needs to be said two to three times a week for the first ten years of marriage—and at least once a week for the rest of marriage. Why? In order to maintain a steady focus on the promises that form the steel framework of the marriage. With this structure in place, it is much more likely that commitment will shape the attitudes of a person, as well as the behavioral expression of those attitudes. If commitment is verbalized regularly over a long period of time, it takes on enormous power.

When I developed a plan for anger management,[3] I originally asked anger mismanagers to prepare a statement about how they wanted to be the next time they were angry and to read it aloud once a week for twenty-six weeks. My clients found this extremely beneficial, but when I raised the frequency of reading to three times a week, the effect on behavior was substantially greater. The same is true of marriage vows. The more we say them, the more we will *live* them.

Undoubtedly, challenging marital problems will arise frequently, but the frequency of the problems is not at all our concern. Our concern centers on the way the problems are managed by the two partners. If they approach each problem with an attitude and demeanor best characterized as loving, honoring, and cherishing to the spouse, the marriage is likely to get stronger rather than weaker. But if the two people bring in selfish attitudes, the marriage will be damaged, and the problems will remain unresolved. Reciting the marital promises on a frequent basis will ensure a maximally fresh and precisely focused set of attitudes.

A FORM FOR MARITAL-VOW REHEARSAL

The most effective way to recite vows on a regular basis is to find a method that makes the process natural, meaningful, and even fun. Every couple I have worked with has had their own unique way of managing this task. Let me tell you about one of them.

Sue and Jim came to my office with all kinds of marital difficulties. In fact they had been separated for a month at the time they called me. We worked through a dozen or more issues over the next few weeks, and they were finally ready to recommit themselves to each other. I suggested the training program I have been describing here.

If you knew Sue and Jim, you would understand how crucial it was for them to stay carefully focused on their promises to each other. Because they both had strong opinions about virtually everything, including each other's behavior, they were constantly in danger of igniting arguments and conflicts. Moreover, their anger-management styles heightened the risk of every interpersonal conflict.

The three of us knew that their vows to love, honor, and cherish each other needed regular expression so that these promises would influence their attitudes and behavior at the moment when marital conflict threatened. When we discussed the need to recite these promises on a regular basis, Sue and Jim came up with a short statement that included every important promise from their marital vows. It went like this: "I will love you when times are good or bad. I will cherish you even if I am upset with you. I will honor you at *all* times. I will never be disloyal to you. And I mean this forever. So help me God."

They didn't leave the house in the morning without saying this to each other. Jim even developed a tune so that he could sing it to Sue. It became a ritual that was full of meaning for both of them. And it had dramatic results. The theme of their lives became "I will love you when times are good or bad." It came to permeate their relationship with each other. It ruled over them even in the middle of their inevitable conflicts. Sue told me many times that the daily verbalization of their promises to each other significantly moderated every disagreement they had.

In fact, exactly one year after beginning this daily promise-making tradition, Jim wrote me a card that said,

Dear Neil,

Sue and I are supremely happy together. Everything changed when we began focusing on our promises to each other. We never tire of telling each other what each of us so loves to hear. Sue says to tell you that she has learned a lot of new ways to cherish me while totally disagreeing with me.

Love, Jim

NEW AND CREATIVE WAYS TO SAY YOUR VOWS

"I will love you when times are good or bad. I will cherish you even if I am upset with you. I will honor you at all times." Every couple can profit from saying these simple words to each other every day. The more each person can find new and creative ways to swear this commitment, the better. For instance, some part of it can be put into a lunch sack, engraved inside a bracelet, scribbled on a refrigerator note in the morning, contained in a love letter, or written in the sky above a football game.

The idea is to recite this vow over and over so that when the rocky times come, as they inevitably will, and when the flat places appear, as they inevitably will, the commitment to love, honor, and cherish will trigger new ideas in the brain about how to hold the marriage together.

Periodic rewrites of the commitment statement will make it even stronger. And new ways of living out the commitment—beyond simply verbalizing it—will wind its meaning around the bedrock of your soul.

We are all creatures of habit. Few habits are more crucial than those associated with living out the commitment vows. We want those habits to be so "bulldozer strong" that they will literally overwhelm any opposition.

In the middle of a marital crisis, when an impulse darts across your brain that says, "Walk out—just get up and leave him," we want the rehearsed response to be "I love you, I will always love you, and I want to find a way to make this work with you." When your brain flashes, "Gore her with some well-chosen words, make her feel as rotten about herself as you can," we want the steady old voice within to sound loud and strong: "I will find a way to cherish you even in this; this will not drive us apart." Such steadiness and maturity in the face of a momentary thunder-and-lightning storm is only possible if the habituated response is deeply rooted in your being through the long years of rehearsal, well before the rain starts pelting you.

COMMITMENT MULTIPLIES MARITAL STRENGTH

I have never known of a marriage that didn't benefit dramatically from a simple exercise designed to help both partners clarify and articulate their promises. Couples often call me for help when their marriages are in terrible trouble. Many psychologists and marriage counselors are contacted as a last resort, just before an attorney is called.

Carolyn and Mike were like that. They were fed up with each other! I agreed to see them on a Saturday because they were worn out from fighting and they were headed to a lawyer on Monday morning to begin divorce proceedings.

Fortunately, they were a perfect case for me—the right ages, the right personal styles, the right backgrounds. Their problems were tough, but we dug in. Together, we began to make some progress, and they agreed to delay calling their attorney. Even though there were huge hurdles to overcome, Mike and Carolyn wanted so much to be married that they worked hard, harder than they ever had, at resolving their differences.

After months of work, their marriage was finally on solid ground. And it still is! They continue to experience times of intense frustration with each other, but now they are deeply immersed in a love that enables them to work through the problems. Like so many couples, Mike and Carolyn crave hearing the other person talk about that special kind of love as they repeat their promises to each other.

I have to tell you that, even today, when I remember one of them finally saying those deep-down, old-fashioned vows to the other, my eyes fill with tears and my throat gets a huge lump in it. I remember how Mike, after all those months of fighting had finally subsided, would look straight at this woman he loved and speak softly: "Carolyn, I will love you when times are good or bad. I will cherish you even if I am upset with you. I will honor you at all times. I will never be disloyal to you. And this is forever. So help me God."

A couple who says this to each other every day is well on their way to a triumphant marriage.

Don't kid yourself. Great marriages are the result of back-breaking work! They simply do not come easily. Two people must be skillful and strong. They need to be tough! Strength and toughness come from reciting over and over: "I will love you when times are good or bad. So help me God."

Chapter Three

THE HONEST TRUTH ABOUT ALL RELATIONSHIPS*

Becky and Dr. Roger Tirabassi

As Roger and I grew up, we both remember our dads making that all-too-familiar statement, "Women! You can't live with them; you can't live without them." We also remember our moms responding to our dads by raising their eyebrows, giving a whimsical look, and retorting, "And men! You can't live with them; you can't live without them."

It's one of the few statements about marriage that both men and women agree on! We acknowledge our need to live with a lifelong mate, but we find that living with them can be difficult.

Our belief is that living with them can also be a joy if we have realistic expectations, prepare for our inevitable struggles, and make the necessary adjustments for our differing personalities and needs.

EVERY COUPLE IS BOUND TO STRUGGLE

The desire to live with them can be traced all the way back to Genesis 2:18, where God said, "It is not good for the man to be alone." As singles, we spent much time and energy looking for a spouse, desiring to fill our need for companionship, closeness, intimacy, and a family. Ironically, those of us who married the person we "just couldn't live without" discovered that our differing

---

personalities and needs, our unique idiosyncrasies, not to mention our personal pasts, made living with them a challenge!

How can we live with them since we can't live without them? Can it be done? Is it possible? Yes. We believe that you can have a successful marriage by making a commitment to understand each other, develop relationship skills, and make wise decisions.

The first thing to acknowledge about marriage is that every couple is bound to struggle! At a conference, we heard Jay Kesler, president of Taylor University, say, "It is not the blowouts that will destroy your marriage, but the slow leaks." We, too, have found that the day-to-day irritations and frustrations can tear apart the foundation of a loving relationship.

A Perfect Example

The following story describes an actual situation that occurred in our home one morning recently. In a span of less than ten minutes, we dealt with the issues of communicating effectively, playing by preestablished rules, maintaining self-control, understanding how differing needs and personalities interact, asking for and granting forgiveness, and focusing on the positive.

As my assistant was taking her lunch break in our kitchen, unknowingly, Roger and I gave her a live demonstration of many of our relationship principles in action.

I was headed outside to the chaise lounge to have my quiet time, and I saw the garden hose sitting out on the back deck. In a split second I thought, *This hose is just waiting for me to step on it or trip over it.* But I was so focused on getting Roger off the deck so I could get started on my quiet time that I didn't take the time to move it. I rationalized that since he had taken it out, it was his responsibility to put it away.

As I turned to go back into the house to pick up my Bible and get a towel to cover the chaise, I proceeded to trip over that hose, stub my big toe, and holler with pain! As I hopped up and down,

I immediately glared at Roger, giving him full "credit" for my current pain. I said, "I just knew this would happen when I saw that you hadn't put the hose away." He smartly responded, "You saw it, thought about it, stepped on it, then you blamed me! What's wrong with this picture?"

Rather than deal any longer with that scenario, I went out to the laundry room to get a towel as my assistant tried not to laugh at me behind her napkin. There I found a dryer full of half done, damp laundry and another pile of clothes lying on the floor. Still upset and aching from stepping on the hose nozzle, I picked up a clean towel, marched back into the kitchen, and barked, "Roger, if you are going to start the laundry, please finish it. Gosh, I go on a trip for three days, leaving everything in its place, and I come back to hoses and clothes just lying all over the place! Let's start a new rule: Don't start any laundry unless you can finish it!"

Roger had another smart reply, which he directed toward my assistant rather than to me. "Becky's always coming up with a new rule. Three weeks ago she went away, and I found a load of laundry in the dryer that was still damp and very wrinkled." He proceeded to tell the rest of his story with dramatic Italian gestures. "I had to put heat on the clothes for another few minutes, just to get all the wrinkles out. Then I had to bring them into the living room, flatten and fold them all, piece by piece." He used grand smoothing and folding gestures to show how very difficult it was, but my assistant does enough of her own laundry to feel little sympathy for this singular instance of Roger's domesticity. He continued, "Then I had to put all of our clothes away and go back to finish the load I was starting simply because Becky didn't finish the laundry before she went away! But now that the clothes are in her way, we have a new rule!" (Roger was squawking about a new rule like the Mad Hatter at his tea party yelling for clean cups!)

This exchange led to a hearty discussion about rules, particularly since we had just written that section of our book. I jokingly suggested that we could add the (laundry and hose) "finish what you start rule" as #14 in our collection of marital rules! But my assistant, Jennifer, informed me that we already *had* a rule #14. Roger had expanded on the rule section in my absence. By that time, we were all laughing hysterically over the ridiculousness of the situation.

Just as things calmed down, we went outside to have our quiet time when Roger noticed Kezi, our big black Labrador retriever, sprawled largely on the lawn. (In fact, just that morning the little neighbor girl screamed aloud, "Look, Mommy, Kezi got fat since I last saw her!") Roger made a comment, "You're just a big stupid dog, Kezi." Even though he said it with a smile in his voice, I jumped on that! I said, "Roger, you broke a rule! You aren't allowed to say 'stupid'!"

Roger replied, "You broke a rule too. You aren't allowed to say, 'You broke a rule,' remember? Besides, have you forgotten? I didn't ask for Kezi. When I agreed to let you get Kezi in the first place, you promised that I wouldn't have to walk her, feed her, or pick up after her! But now I do all of those things all of the time!"

Well, that was an exaggeration. Roger does help with Kezi when I can't do it (and he does love her, no matter what he says).

My assistant quietly piped in from the kitchen, "Roger, remember what you said to Becky before, 'What's wrong with this picture?' Did you really believe that you could get a dog and never have to walk her, feed her, or pick up after her?" Her comment didn't need an answer, and once again, we were all laughing!

By the way, twenty-four hours later the laundry was folded, but on the couch, waiting to be put away, and the hose was still lying in the same place on the deck, and Roger had to take Kezi for a walk that morning.

We chose this illustration because it's an example of a common situation in most homes. Our goal has been to recognize the daily, inevitable misunderstandings as they occur, not be surprised by them, but even learn to manage them!

EVERY RELATIONSHIP GOES THROUGH PHASES

In addition to understanding that every couple will struggle, it is equally important to recognize that your relationship will go through phases, and some of the phases are more difficult than others.

Phase 1: Infatuation

Most relationships begin with infatuation. The Infatuation Phase is characterized by an increased heart rate, a "felt" excitement, and a tendency to see only the good in the other person. In this phase, the weaknesses of the other are minimized, perhaps not even seen at all! Each person seeks to please the other in big and small ways, for example, by giving a rose, opening a car door, buying gifts, or writing notes. During this phase, little is expected by the giver in return for what is given, and whatever is reciprocated is met with adulation! The energy expended in this first relationship phase comes naturally, with very little effort, and with a minimum of emotional drain. Love feels unconditional.

Phase 2: Reality

Then reality hits! At some point during the Reality Phase, both people begin to see the other person's faults and personality weaknesses. They are acutely aware of the other's selfish side, insensitivity, and noncaring behavior. They no longer see the other as Mr. or Miss Perfect. The bubble has officially been burst in this phase! Where once there was an increased heart rate, now the pulse is normal. Ideally, this phase occurs during courtship. But if they are married, it is during this stage that the wife secretly concedes, "I didn't marry a knight in shining armor, " and the husband reflects, "She may not be the girl of my dreams."

These stages will be a little different for everyone. Married couples have a responsibility to get through this phase. Single people have the option to reevaluate their relationship at this stage. Some people become so disillusioned during the Reality Phase that they break off the relationship. Many people never even get to the third stage of a successful relationship because they bail or step out at the Reality Phase.

Phase 3: Adjustment

The third and final phase of a loving or effective relationship is called the Adjustment Phase. At this point, both parties are committed to resolving their differences in mutually compromising and satisfactory ways. During this phase, acts of love are not always done because one feels like doing them, but because they are the right and loving things to do. In the Adjustment Phase the couple must put extra effort into doing things that came naturally to them in the Infatuation Phase.

During this final phase, the couple must be able to endure their pain and disappointments. In the Adjustment Phase, there is more focus on forgiveness, reconciliation, sacrifice, conflict resolution, and intentional listening. These acts of love will help the couple through a lifetime of relationship struggles.

CURRENT RELATIONSHIPS ARE AFFECTED BY OUR PAST

The third fact about relationships is that they are affected by our past. In most relationships, there is an area of conflict that occurs over and over. (Sometimes there are several areas!) When we examine the conflicting areas, we often find a person, crisis, or experience from our past that is affecting the way we are reacting in our current relationship. The influence from our past creates thoughts, feelings, or behaviors within us that can contaminate and damage our relationships. Some of these include distrust, insecurity, inadequacies, and fear of or the need to control.

For example, Bill has an outgoing and gregarious personality. He is very friendly, but at times almost overbearing. In his family of origin, he didn't receive much attention, encouragement, or affirmation. Therefore, as an adult, he has an insatiable need for approval, affirmation, and attention.

In his relationships with women, Bill's behavior appears to be flirtatious. He is unwilling to admit that this behavior is inappropriate, and he gets angry if his wife, Sue, mentions anything about it. Sue gives Bill a lot of attention, but that is not enough for him. His need for approval and affirmation keeps him searching for more attention.

Bill is attempting to fill a void that he feels inside, but his behavior is hurting Sue. He needs to understand that the effects of his past have created this insatiable need within him that has the power to damage his relationship with his wife. Because his compulsion to fill this void is so powerful, Bill loses perspective in all of his relationships.

Bill's need for more than normal amounts of approval, affirmation, and attention results in his flirtatious behavior. Sue doesn't appreciate his actions, and the effects of her past intensify her feelings of jealousy. Because Sue grew up not feeling special or significant, Bill's behavior hurts his wife more deeply than it would hurt most women (not that this behavior wouldn't hurt anyone). Because of her past, she struggles with strong feelings of insecurity and lack of love. His behavior frightens her. She chooses to withdraw from him to protect her feelings. He then receives less attention and searches for it even more in the wrong places.

Taking Practical Steps

You can take practical steps to overcome your past experiences.

1. The first step to take to better your current relationship is to become aware of the negative thoughts, feelings, and behaviors that might be a result of your past. Do any from this list pertain to you?

> Need for unusual amounts of affirmation, affection, and/or approval
> Feeling rejected
> Being critical
> Not feeling valued, special
> Feeling abandoned
> Difficulty in trusting
> Hypersensitivity to anger
> Need to please
> Fearful
> Perfectionism
> Not feeling accepted
> Inadequacy
> Need to control
> Feelings of insecurity
> Secrecy
> Poor self-image
> Excessive spending

After you have identified a few of the thoughts, feelings, or behaviors on the list, recall the incidents from childhood that could have precipitated your reactions. To reflect on specific situations, you might want to set aside time to journal. During this time, write down the incident as you remember it. Include your feelings, thoughts, and reactions, as well as how the incident affected you. Then you can turn this reflection time into a prayer, asking God to help you forgive those who have hurt you and to bring healing to your past.

2. The second step is to acknowledge that your past experiences are hurting your present relationship. In doing this, you are helping your partner understand you better. Realizing that the current struggle is not just about the present circumstances diffuses the intensity of the current conflict. The admission and understanding of your weaknesses, as well as the influences of your past, lead to a greater sensitivity toward loved ones.

The following situation demonstrates how the past can hinder a current relationship. Joe hides his financial difficulties from important people in his life, especially his wife, Jane. He has purchased a number of items that he can't afford. These purchases put him in greater debt, but he doesn't want to share the severity of the situation with anyone, fearing that others might think he is inadequate and incompetent.

Joe's perception of himself as inadequate began as a child when he was ridiculed by his peers for being short and nonathletic. To counter his present inadequate feelings, he spends money excessively. Material possessions give him a sense of power and success. But his overspending has severely damaged his relationship with his wife because he has created a huge debt for them. He can no longer even provide necessities for her.

Hence the dilemma: Having been criticized in childhood, Joe developed a poor self-image and a feeling of powerlessness. As an adult, Joe numbs his pain by buying things, even though he can't afford them. Though spending money initially makes him feel powerful, it deeply and negatively affects his relationship with his wife. When Joe took the time to acknowledge that his past was affecting his relationship with his wife, it helped him to make some positive changes.

When we don't understand and resolve our past, we search for ways to cope with or numb our pain. The ways that we cope or numb can include the inappropriate use of money, sexuality, alcohol, drugs, or work. These can often and easily turn into addictions. In his counseling practice, Roger has found that most people with these addictions have unresolved family-of-origin issues. These unresolved issues can destroy marriages and families. *Understanding our past—and taking responsible steps to change—is fundamental to experiencing successful relationships.*

3. Another very helpful step we encourage you to take is to join a small group or support group. Roger and I have joined support groups, and we recommend the small group experience to you as well. Small groups and support groups are places where you can identify your issues and receive encouragement to work through them. Several friends attend Alcoholics Anonymous (AA), 12 Step groups, and growth groups. These groups differ from Bible study groups because they are designed to be places to honestly confess our shortcomings to one another.

The concept of attending small groups has been widely accepted in southern California for a number of years. Roger's friend, Ron Jensen, has developed and encouraged Spiritual Growth Groups, which focus on applying biblical principles in support group settings while at the same time providing accountability. Single and married men and women discuss the thoughts, feelings, and behaviors that hinder their relationships. In a safe setting, it has been remarkable to see how many men and women have been vulnerable, transparent, and willing to change.

EVERY RELATIONSHIP
REQUIRES MOTIVATION TO SUCCEED

What motivates a couple or an individual to press on when confronting the truth about relationships? The knowledge that

- Every couple is bound to struggle;
- Every relationship goes through phases;

- Current relationships are affected by our past.

What keeps both partners committed to each other during difficulty? What makes them fight for their relationship? What motivates a person to face the pain or disappointment in the relationship without giving up? Every person is motivated differently.

For some people, it is their *strong willpower*. They are actually motivated by their determination to never fail or quit. These people are often very disciplined and just won't accept failure. But self-will or inner motivation doesn't work for everyone. Some people have no trouble quitting. In fact, they often give up too soon.

Others are motivated to stay in a relationship for *fear of what people might think of them* if they ended a relationship, quit, or left. Although on the surface this doesn't appear to be a good motivator, it can have the positive effect of pushing the couple to discover better ways to relate to each other and avoid breakup.

Still other people are motivated to press through pain because of their *convictions* to keep their word. For example, if they went to the altar and said, "For better or for worse, for richer or poorer, until death do us part," they have made a verbal commitment in front of others and are determined to keep their promises.

Many are motivated to work through their pain because of their *spiritual commitments*. For example, some Christians stay married because they adhere to the biblical principles that "God hates divorce" and "what God has joined together, let no man separate." Their religious belief is their motivational factor.

Couples with children who are struggling in their relationship are motivated to resolve their differences *for the sake of the children*. They don't want their kids to be uprooted, moved to different homes, split up during the holidays, or forced to choose between parents. These people are driven to work out the difficulties in their relationship because they don't want their children to lose their sense of family, unity, stability, or security.

Having spent many years as a youth worker, Roger has seen and counseled hundreds of kids from divorced homes who have experienced incredibly painful feelings. He has watched as they were forced to make many difficult adjustments *simply* because their parents weren't motivated to persevere through the struggles in the Adjustment Phase of their relationship.

Certainly, where there is abuse or unfaithfulness, reconciliation is very difficult and a more complex process. But even in those cases, it might be possible, though much work will have to be done to save the relationship.

The following statements have been used to motivate married couples. Our hope is that by reviewing this list, you will identify thoughts that can motivate you to work through the struggles of your relationship.

1. It is unacceptable for us to fail.
2. I am determined not to quit.
3. I know that blessings will follow if I don't give up.
4. I might experience great pain if I stop trying.
5. I might leave a positive legacy if I just press on.
6. I might create great pain for my children if I leave now.
7. I probably will face this same problem with someone else in the future.
8. I am aware that nothing great was ever achieved without sacrifice.
9. I have the conviction of my own word.
10. All couples struggle; this is not abnormal.
11. I do not want to disappoint or let other people down.
12. My spiritual commitment will help me get through this difficult time.

Of course, there are less-noble motivations for remaining committed to a struggling relationship. Some people are paralyzed with the fear of facing the unknown, or they are unwilling to give up financial security supplied by the spouse. Though these motivations are not as healthy as others, they keep a couple together as they work through their struggles.

Wise People Seek Counsel

Perhaps even as you read this chapter, you feel too tired or discouraged to press on. You believe that you have done everything in your power to bring resolve. You've gone to counseling, prayer services, pastoral care, and therapy, and you've talked with friends—but nothing worked. If you are married, while we empathize with you, we must ultimately say, "Don't quit!" We believe that too many couples prematurely leave their relationship without considering the cost, or without turning over every rock possible to find resolve or resolution.

For those of you who have tried a counselor, yet haven't found help, try another. Get help, and get good help. If you are at an impasse, rather than give up, we suggest that you meet with a different professional Christian counselor or psychologist. Roger has seen many people receive help only after their fifth try! Sometimes the hearts take that long to soften. Perhaps one counselor is simply a better fit than another.

WHAT'S THE HONEST TRUTH ABOUT ALL RELATIONSHIPS?

We hope this chapter has helped you understand the following three truths about relationships:

1. Struggles are common to relationships.
2. All relationships go through phases.
3. Your past affects your present.

If you and your spouse can accept these truths and identify those things that will motivate you to stay committed to each other no matter what, it will make *living with them* much more satisfying.

Chapter Four

MEMO TO MOM AND DAD: THE KIDS AND THE JOB DON'T COME FIRST!*

Dr. Kevin Leman

As a counselor and therapist, I have the privilege and responsibility of observing life behind closed doors. In any given year, I am invited into many different family circles, where people share with me their most precious possessions—their personal lives, their hopes, their fears, their problems, and their pain.

As part of my counseling, I ask a lot of questions. One of my favorite approaches is to talk to husbands and wives separately and ask, "What are your spouse's priorities?"

When I ask the wife this question, almost invariably I hear that the number-one priority in her husband's life is his job. Then she might describe his number-two priority as "the family." Not infrequently, however, she says that his golf game or some other hobby is number two and that the family comes in a distant third. Some women say, "I guess I come in around fourth or fifth."

Until recently, when I asked husbands, "What is your wife's number-one priority?" they typically said, "Oh, the children. Marge is a great mother, a great homemaker." In recent years, however, I'm hearing husbands tell me that the family isn't necessarily always number one with their wives. Now wives are being torn between the family and "their career." When I ask a husband or wife about priorities, the answer I am hoping to hear, but seldom

---

*Adapted from Dr. Kevin Leman, *Keeping Your Family Together When the World Is Falling Apart* (New York: Delacorte, 1992). Used by permission.

do, is that the number-one priority for the wife is her husband and the number-one priority for the husband is his wife. When I suggest this to my clients, they look at me strangely, as if that idea were something from the distant past—back when they were dating, perhaps. Don't I realize that, once married, one's priorities have to change? Jobs and careers take precedence, and when children arrive, they *really* take precedence.

The concept of "putting each other first" is foreign to most married couples. It just isn't practical—there are too many responsibilities, too many urgent tasks that have to be done each day.

TRAPPED IN THE TYRANNY OF THE URGENT

I counsel a lot of couples who think they are suffering from money problems, in-laws, "strong-willed" children, or "the other woman." All these symptoms may be present, but the real problem centers on what has commonly become known as "the tyranny of the urgent." I'm not sure who coined that phrase, but a man named Charles Hummel used it to title a small booklet he wrote to point out that there is a real difference between the urgent and the important.

As Hummel was talking to the manager of a cotton mill one day, the much older and experienced man said, "Your greatest danger is letting the urgent things crowd out the important."[1] Hummel realized that the man had put the whole subject of priorities in a nutshell. *Everybody* lives somewhere between doing what is urgent and doing what is important.

In the families I come in contact with, it seems that the "urgent" things scream the loudest to be done: getting the kids up, packing their lunches, getting them to the school bus, getting down to work yourself, stopping to pick up groceries on the way home, throwing dinner together. Then, after dinner, you get to relax with a pile of monthly bills that need paying or clothes that need washing or ironing.

Unfortunately, while you're covering all these urgent bases, the important things go undone. As General and later President Eisenhower once said, "Urgent matters are seldom important; important matters are seldom urgent!" One problem is that the important things are seldom those that really need to be done right now, today, or even this week. You can always put off writing or phoning a friend you haven't contacted in several months. It's always easy to find an excuse for delaying the start of your diet or your latest "I've got to quit smoking" campaign. And it's all just too easy to put "time for each other" aside because there just doesn't seem to be any.

"DR. LEMAN, I'M GOING BONKERS!"

A harried-looking woman, dragging her leg as if she had some sort of neurological disorder, limped into my office one day. As she plopped down on the sofa, I noted that the reason for her odd gait was an eighteen-month-old child who was clinging to her skirt like a leech.

The lady's first words were, "Can you help me, Dr. Leman? *I'm going bonkers!*"

It turned out that this lady's plaintive remark eventually inspired the title of a book I wrote to help overwhelmed women: *Bonkers: Why Women Get Stressed Out and What They Can Do About It.*[2]

The lady who admitted to going "bonkers" was a classic prototype of the stressed-out woman. She was trying hard to be a good mother to four children while balancing everything else as well: her husband, a full-time job, and three or four other assignments she had taken on from the PTA, her church, and the cerebral palsy campaign. Her story is the story of so many women who wind up in my office.

The woman who is a candidate for Bonkersville comes trudging home from her job and fixes dinner, and after hubby and the children have all eaten she cleans up the kitchen. Then she stops to pick up the family room and living room as well.

Next, she irons something for tomorrow, packs some lunches, and finally heads for the bedroom, where she hopes to read a few pages of her mystery novel or turn on the eleven o'clock news. There she is, propped up on her pillows, reaching for her book or the *TV Guide* and he walks in with a look that reminds her of Pavlov's dog and the power of operant conditioning. She spots his salivating smile and the glint in his eyes and groans, "Oh, no . . . not, not, not—no, no, no—*not one more chore!*"

Poor hubby. He doesn't realize it, but his wife has just erected her own little neon sign that reads, *Don't Even Think of Parking Here.* Most women would rather scrub the toilet than engage in sex at 10:55 at night after working all day, cooking dinner, cleaning up, putting the kids to bed, and making sure everything is ready for tomorrow.

Our stressed-out woman doesn't realize it, but she is definitely a victim of the tyranny of the urgent. The urgent tasks of her day have crowded out the important things—including hubby and his salivating smile. Of course, since hubby hasn't done his part, all he'll get to do tonight is salivate. He could have ensured himself a much warmer welcome to bed if he had helped her clean up the kitchen, pick up the house, and get the kids bathed and down for the night. But he was too busy watching the Monday night gladiators of the gridiron. After all, there are certain things in his life that are "urgent" too.

Frankly, I talk to a lot of women who succumb to the tyranny of the urgent while their husbands succumb to selfishness or just not being aware of the situation.

If there is a message I want to communicate, it is this:

ATTENTION ALL HUSBANDS!

YOUR WIFE CAN'T KEEP YOUR FAMILY TOGETHER
ALL BY HERSELF.

YOU MUST PLAY AN ACTIVE ROLE IN HELPING SORT
OUT THE URGENT AND THE IMPORTANT AND THEN
DO YOUR SHARE OF BOTH.

Lately, I'm talking to more and more working wives who are rebelling against the tyranny of the urgent. They have tried to "have it all," but now they are deciding that they really prefer to give some of it back. They find themselves in the classic two-career family where both they and their husbands have stressful full-time jobs. Then these wives have to come home to "start their second job," which leaves them exhausted and depressed most of the time. Like our "going bonkers" wife described above, they wind up just too tired for sex—or much of anything else that could remotely resemble building a strong marriage relationship.

FULL SPEED AHEAD ON THE MOMMY TRACK

There isn't any simple answer. The working-wife movement is not going away—in fact, it's proliferating. Betty Friedan has described the 1990s as a time when "women will have new economic power" because companies will have to compete to get women. Nearly 70 percent of new jobs will be filled by women and minorities.[3] An increasing number of husbands will at least admit they should help more with the kids and the housework, but in reality few of them follow through and do it with any regularity.

Recognizing that something has to give, employers are now offering all kinds of options to working moms who are forced to come to grips with reality regarding the care of their families. Among these options are innovations like extended leave after having a child, flexible scheduling or flextime, job sharing, and even telecommuting.

One other thing some working moms can consider is "sequencing"—leaving their jobs for a few years and then trying to come back and continue their careers. Some women have made this work with no apparent damage to their careers. For example, Sandra Day O'Connor, a justice of the Supreme Court, took five years off from her law career and cared for her three children. Later, she was able to return to full-time employment as Arizona's assistant attorney general, and from there she rose all the way to the highest court in the land.[4]

Bully for Justice O'Connor, but a lot of other women can tell you that sequencing has its drawbacks. They aren't able to return to their old job and continue the upward climb uninterrupted. In many cases, they lose ground on the career ladder, and sometimes it means losing a choice position and having to start over at the very bottom or in a completely new field.

I know of increasing numbers of women who are bailing out of stress-ridden executive positions in corporations and businesses and opting for the entrepreneurial route by matching up with a friend to start small businesses in their homes. It's their way of getting back their equilibrium on the balance beam of life. They keep one high heel in the business world, but they firmly plant a Reebok at home, where they are more able to spend their time according to the needs and priorities of their families.

All these options for working wives and mothers fall under a broader label called "alternative work schedules," a term coined by Felice Schwartz, founder and president of Catalyst, a nonprofit organization devoted to advancing women's careers, in an article she wrote concerning women in management for the *Harvard Business Review*.[5] Ms. Schwartz's premise was that employers have to face reality and identify two separate groups of women employees: (1) the high-potential, "my career comes first" women, most of whom are probably childless and willing to devote unlimited time to their jobs; (2) the lower-potential, "my family is important too" women who have children and want to spend as much time as they can in rearing and nurturing them.

Critics quickly jumped on Schwartz's concept and labeled it the "Mommy Track." They pointed out that anybody on the Mommy Track is on the B team down at work. Because she has made it known that she can't give it all to the corporation, she definitely can't have it all as far as advancement and rewards are concerned. Men, of course, will leave all the Mommy-Trackers in the dust as the women drag their second-class status around like a millstone about their necks.

I'm sure all that is true in certain organizations, but as a psychologist who talks with burned-out superwomen all the time, I can only say that something has to give and choices have to be made. Those who criticize the so-called Mommy Track are clearly stating what they think a woman's priorities should be. Career must come first, and the fast track must be pursued right to the top. Of course, once the woman gets to the top, she may be exhausted, possibly ready for the local funny farm, and feeling so drenched in guilt about neglecting her family that she can't enjoy any of the fruits of her labor.

Or she may be so stressed out that she falls ill—sometimes very seriously ill. According to a letter written to the *New York Times* by Dr. Paul Rosch, the president of the American Institute of Stress, there is real reason to believe that the sharp increase in the death rate from breast cancer in young and middle-aged white women is traceable to the stress these women undergo on the job as they "enter a male dominated workforce that fails to fulfill the promises of women's liberation efforts."

According to Dr. Rosch, "Job stress is also associated with 100 percent increase in heart attacks in certain classes of working women, especially those in occupations where one cannot express anger or that require a great deal of responsibility but little deci-sion-making. Other illness syndromes and behavioral problems, such as smoking, alcoholism, substance abuse and obesity, appear to be consequences of work-related stress."[6]

It is apparent that for many women, joining the workforce has meant joining the rat race. They may not have wanted it to be that way, but they are trapped in the rat race and they should never forget: *When the rat race is over, you're still a rat.*

In other words, if you are willingly sucked into the rat race and let running that race dominate your life, you have made your choice. Your priority is plain. The rat race is most important to you, and whether you like it or not, you have chosen to live life as mindlessly as a rat on a wheel, going around and around but really not getting anywhere as far as what counts is concerned. And what counts is people. No matter how important a career might be—and I am fully aware that a career is very important to many women as well as men—a career should never come ahead of people close to you.

"THE AIR FORCE DOESN'T COME FIRST"

So far, I may sound as if I think the woman ought to do all the choosing of "alternatives" while the man can keep pouring himself into his job, Monday-night football, and getting his handicap below ten. On the contrary, I think it is the husbands of our nation who face some serious choices regarding their work and alternative lifestyles. And they'd better make them fast, because for many fam-ilies time may be running out. I talk to more and more women who are considering the option of going it alone instead of carrying hus-bands who only add more stress to their lives. One divorce summed it up by saying, "I used to have five children—now I only have four."

I'll never forget the air force colonel who was in the audience when I spoke to a group of air force wives at the base chapel. After

I concluded my talk, which featured numerous suggestions that men ought to be doing more around the house, particularly if their wives are working, I opened the session for questions. I didn't know the colonel was in the audience, but that changed when he towered to his feet and said in a loud military tone, "Doctor, could I just say one thing?"

"Of course," I invited. How could a civilian psychologist turn down a colonel who wanted the floor?

"Young man, it seems to me that you don't understand the air force. Because, you see, when a woman marries into the air force, the woman knows right off the bat, the air force must come first."

The colonel went on to elaborate, and I let him drone for maybe sixty to ninety seconds before interrupting him.

"Excuse me, sir, I really do believe I understand your air force. But the fact is, if you die tonight, your air force will have someone filling your shoes by 0800 tomorrow morning."

It seemed that every woman in the room rose to her feet to give me a standing ovation while the colonel slowly sank back into his seat, shot down in the flames of his own reality. He had nicely provided a vivid illustration of the point I was trying to make: a job is not everything. No matter what position anyone holds, that position can be filled by somebody else. But at home, this isn't true. When you take on the commitment of marriage and parenting, *there is no one who can fill your shoes at home.* If you're off doing something else, you leave a gap that cannot be filled.

As I have worked with men in counseling situations, I have learned that I have to convince them of their importance to their families. In addition, I always have to demonstrate what's in it for them. After all, that's how a man thinks.

So I work hard at explaining to husbands how their sex lives will improve 300 percent if they'll just take time to do the little things in life, like taking out the garbage without being asked, taking the kids to school, being more attentive to their mothers-in-law—or possibly most important: changing their schedules. In addition, although it's hard for them to believe it, I point out that man does not live by sex alone. Besides being males, men are *human*. When a man is on his deathbed, looking back on his corporate achievements won't bring much comfort. The human spirit has a different list of priorities. Did he take time to play with and really *know* his kids? Did he make some real friends, or did he just pick partners for racquetball or golf? Did he ever get to know his wife as his friend—the best friend he could possibly have? Did he take time to appreciate the beauty of God's handiwork? Did he take time to enjoy life, or did he just put in his time?

ALL YOU HAVE TO INVEST IS YOUR TIME

I'm not telling men anything I haven't had to learn myself— several times. It's interesting how life reteaches you certain lessons. When our little surprise package, Hannah, arrived a few years ago, I was forty-four and Sande was forty-two. Sande had told me she was pregnant while we were eating at a fast-food restaurant just before Christmas. I can remember letting out a war whoop of joy, which was later countered by a few pangs of chagrin. After all, what were two people in their forties doing having another baby? We had three already: Holly, fifteen; Krissy, fourteen; and Kevie, nine. How could the champion of Reality Discipline have slipped up so badly?[7]

Counselor, heal thyself flashed through my mind, but joy was still my predominant reaction. Maybe I was unconsciously happy about getting a second chance to try some things I hadn't done all that well with the first three.

As you would guess, Hannah's birth brought changes to the Leman household. For one thing, I had to make some changes, because I couldn't expect Sande to attend to the new baby and do everything she had been doing before. Among many other things,

I altered my work schedule so I could take over driving our older kids to the school they attend, some ten miles away. That cost me some early-morning appointments at the office, and it also meant reducing income that we sorely needed at the time.

What I keep telling men is that all that any of us have is dominion over our time and how we spend it. I go to psychologists' conventions on occasion, and always during the sessions on how to conduct a private practice the seminar leaders keep saying one thing: "All you have to sell is your time."

That piece of wisdom doesn't just apply to running a business. It applies to being part of a marriage and a family too. *Selling* time is only part of it. There is also the area of *investing* time, and what better investment of your time can you make than in your family?

THE CASE OF THE SEETHING SURGEON

I recall a physician—a dyed-in-his-surgeon's-gown workaholic making well over a half-million dollars a year—who came to see me because his wife had told him she was fed up with being neglected and alone all the time with the children. She was ready to walk out if something didn't change, and fast.

As this man described his schedule and daily routine, it was quickly apparent that he was married to his job, locked in to commitments, and that he was telling himself lies. One lie centered on bringing new people into his practice and supposedly making his workload go down. He had just brought in a new surgeon, but his own practice had only gotten bigger because he was simply becoming more and more in demand for his skills.

His wife's outburst had taken him totally by surprise. She had been supermom, raising the three kids, providing a gracious home, keeping everything under control—everything but her own feelings, which had slowly deteriorated as she spent night after night eating with the children while he was still down at the office or hospital, hard at work.

In this case, the wife did not work outside the home—with an income of a half-million dollars a year, she didn't have to. And because this doctor was the sole provider of the income in his home, he could tell himself the lie that he was doing all this for his wife and children. He was beating his head against the wall for her and the kids. But now she was fed up. She wanted more than the nice home and being able to buy whatever she wanted. In short, she wanted *him*.

But when he did get home, he would head straight for the liquor cabinet, pour himself a drink, and try to unwind from the day. He wanted no part of the children—or of her, for that matter. He just wanted to be left in peace. He worked like this five days a week, up to sixty, seventy, and even eighty hours. He was off weekends, yes, but all he did was sit and stare at TV, trying to recharge his batteries for Monday mornings.

This man was so stressed out that he paced my office like a big cat. When I asked him to take a seat on the well-worn couch where so many people sit and tell me their problems, he snatched up one of the smaller pillows and started punching it. With tears streaming down his face, he told me what it was like to be so in demand, so indispensable in the lives of so many people. He also told me that he didn't necessarily like some of these people. He had to be nice, but if he had his druthers, he felt like kicking some of them right in the teeth.

This doctor was so uptight, he was starting to worry about how well he could function in the operating room, and now his wife was ready to leave him to boot. What did I suggest?

"Why don't you try using Reality Discipline on your marriage?" I suggested.

"What do you mean?" he asked.

"Well, it's obvious that you have a five-day-a-week schedule that is eating you alive. Why don't you cut back to three days a week for office visits and surgery, and spend the other two with your family?"

"But I'm needed," he protested. "I don't see how I can cut back."

"Oh, of course you can cut back. Just call your secretary and have her take the pen and cross out Mondays and Fridays. That leaves you with Tuesdays, Wednesdays, and Thursdays, unless there are real emergencies at other times."

"I'm still not sure how I can cram it all into three days," he continued to protest.

Now we were getting down to the real problem. The surgeon really didn't want to cut back on his workload. In his high-powered circles, that would be considered very poor form, and other hardworking surgeons would start to look—and wonder. In a word, his self-esteem would be on the line.

"I realize a man's self-esteem is deeply affected by his work," I told him. "We like to think we're indispensable, and we've got to do more and more to prove it. It's hard to accept the fact that no one is indispensable—at least, not on the job. What I hope I can get you to understand is that where you're really indispensable is at home, and you're not there. If you lay Reality Discipline on your situation, you will realize that there will be consequences if you don't cut back. It seems to me that your choice is rather simple. Cut back on your work, or lose your wife and your family. Do you want to pay that kind of price?"

The stressed-out surgeon looked at me for several seconds, weighing his pride against losing his family. Finally he sat back on the couch and I could almost see the tightly wound spring inside of him start to uncoil just a little.

"Well, I guess I can give it a try. I love what I do, but I love my wife and children too. I don't want to lose them."

It took several more sessions with the surgeon and his wife to get things squared away. But eventually he did cut back. It meant cutting his huge income, but he adjusted to that as well. And they're making it. He's beginning to become reacquainted with his wife and his children. He has also developed a genuine friendship with another surgeon who works at the same hospital, and the families have been getting together. He takes walks whenever he can to relax between surgeries. With tiny baby steps, he's beginning to really enjoy life.

Above all, he has learned that Reality Discipline does work if you're willing to do two things: Face reality, and then discipline yourself and the situation.

SOME HUSBANDS ARE TAKING THE DADDY TRACK

Obviously, the surgeon's story is not representative of the vast majority who do not make over a half-million dollars a year and who cannot afford to cut their workload and salary by thirty or forty percent. What the surgeon *does* illustrate, however, is an attitude that men, especially, must develop if they want to join with their wives in keeping the family intact.

This attitude goes by an old-fashioned term called *humility*. Being humble means realizing that the world does not revolve around your needs and desires. Instead, being a husband and father automatically places you in a new category—that of a servant-leader who fully realizes that the whole is indeed greater than any of its parts, and you must do your part to make the whole—your family—go.

Again, if the husband and wife agree that their first priority is keeping their marriage and family strong, then *both* of them should be willing to bend, shift, or switch. Not to be outdone by the women on the Mommy Track, increasing numbers of men are switching to the Daddy Track as they take alternative career paths of their own in order to become more involved in their families, particularly rearing the children. I read about and talk to more and more men who are giving up promotions, forgoing pay raises, and sacrificing "status" down at work so they can take on a major share of the parenting and homemaking chores that used to be mostly their wives' domain.

In many firms, men go beyond simply wishing they could be with their families more. They take the big step and put their careers on hold.

- A lab technician refuses to work extra hours and weekends so he can spend more time with his kids, and his boss lets him know that "science can't be nine-to-five to be significant."
- A magazine editor quits his job to spend more time with his disabled daughter.
- An account executive forgoes a promotion because his preschool children require more attention.

In one way or another, all these fathers are saying, "I'm not going to do to my kids what my dad did to me. I don't want to be just a paycheck to them."[8]

There are many ways to take the Daddy Track. I recall reading about a football coach at a smaller college who was offered a choice position as head coach at a major school on the East Coast. At first he said he was interested, but when decision time came, he turned it down, saying, "My wife and I have really thought this over, and we've decided that the best thing for our family is to stay where we are."

If you know anything about football coaches, you understand the significance of this man's remark. There is, perhaps, no more ambitious breed than the football coach, many of whom "sleep at 'the office'" during the season because there just isn't time to go home. They're just too busy watching films, holding meetings, and planning strategy. And what I especially like about this coach's remark is that he freely admitted that he had consulted *with his wife* and they had made the decision together to pass up the big-time opportunity and stay in the smaller town, where their kids were firmly rooted, in order to give them the best opportunity to grow up without disruption and confusion.

In another case, I was counseling an architect who decided to put his own career on hold to allow his wife to go back to school. He was fortunate enough to be self-employed and working at home. And so he was able to cut way back on his own work to play Mr. Mom for two years while his wife finished her degree in education.

It's hard to say if the Daddy Track phenomenon will catch hold in major waves. Some critics think it's doubtful that large numbers of men will choose to break out of the more time-honored, traditional roles. One observer—a teacher of parenting courses for almost twenty years—believes that fewer men are putting their families ahead of their jobs today than they did five years ago.[9]

We could argue the pros and cons of the Daddy Track, and the Mommy Track for that matter, but what really counts is one word: *priorities*. When a husband and wife sit down and work out their priorities, then they can make hard decisions about what track each of them is to follow.

DISCIPLINES FOR CHOOSING PRIORITIES

When you choose priorities, you are always dealing with at least two questions: *if* and w*hen*. First, you must decide if you want to do something at all. Once you decide that it is to be done sometime, the next question is *when*. To decide when to do various tasks people sometimes use the ABC approach. To use the ABC system, you take your "to do" list and rate each item as follows:

A = "must do immediately"
B = "should do very soon"

C = "could do some time"

If you're like most people, you'll wind up with quite a few A's, several Bs, and a few Cs. Some people sometimes wind up with all A's, or so they want to believe. Or all of their urgent tasks—the daily routine that just doesn't seem to be able to wait—wind up in the A's. And the important tasks that have a much greater long-range effect on the family wind up in the Bs and even the Cs.

Prioritizing your life is never simple. In *The Road Less Traveled,* Scott Peck observes that solving life's problems involves four basic disciplines:

1. delaying gratification,
2. accepting responsibility,
3. dedicating yourself to being honest and facing the truth, and
4. becoming balanced.

I couldn't agree more, because these four basic tools are Reality Discipline in a nutshell. Unfortunately, when many people choose their priorities, they often take a different route:

- Instead of delaying gratification, they want instant comfort. It's the pleasure principle revisited. The young couple buys the BMW only three years after getting out of grad school. They can't afford it yet, but all their friends are already on their second BMW, and besides, they worked hard and they "deserve it."
- Instead of accepting responsibility, they want to avoid it. Two prime examples that come to mind are the increasing number of divorced or estranged fathers who fail to support their children and the increasing number of college graduates who have defaulted on their student loans. No matter how responsible people think they are, the proof can often be found in how they handle their finances.

• Instead of becoming balanced, they overwork, overeat, or overuse something they shouldn't be using at all. The real estate broker puts in his sixty to seventy hours per week and takes out a membership at the health club, where he spends another ten to fifteen hours, turning fitness into a masochistic ordeal. Meanwhile, his wife is home getting her workouts by handling the children alone every night.

IF THE FOUNDATION ISN'T RIGHT, THE FAMILY CRUMBLES

Not long ago, we sold our home and built a new one just a mile or two away in the arroyos of north Tucson. The contractor who oversaw the building of our house was without question a firstborn child. How do I know? One major clue was his meticulous concern over details. One morning I stopped by the job site at 5:30 A.M. because it would be my only chance to look things over before leaving on a trip. To my surprise, there was Gary.

"I can't believe you're here at five-thirty in the morning," I said in surprise. "The sun's not even up yet."

"Kevin," Gary replied, "it doesn't make much difference if I'm here for a lot of the things that go into your house, but the one thing I have learned is that this is the time I need to be on the spot. This is the day we put in the foundation, and if the foundation isn't right, nothing else is going to be right, either."

Somehow I think there's a parable for families somewhere in Gary's statement. The foundation of every family is the husband and wife. If they don't make that foundation their first priority, then everything else will receive too much, or too little, attention.

If you're really interested in keeping your family together, your first decision should not be about what to do with or for the children. Frankly, most parents are doing too much for their children already.

Your first decision must be to do something for yourselves for Mom and Dad, the basic husband-and-wife unit of the family, around which everything must revolve. I repeat, the children are *not* the center of the family. You and your spouse are the center, and if the center of your marriage doesn't hold, everything else (your family) is going to fly apart.

As I mentioned, a good plan for prioritizing is to label things *A*—must do, *B*—should do, or *C*—can do. But over and above that, you should label your marriage *AAA*—must do. In other words, your marriage is the top priority of them all. In fact, your marriage is much more than a "must do." *It's do or disintegrate.*

If your marriage is coming in a distant second or third or fourth behind a lot of other "priorities," you need to grapple with reality. And reality says that if you don't start doing things differently, you have an excellent chance of becoming one more statistic, one more small part of the giant national average that says a marriage lasts some seven years and is gone.

In a word, *you must prioritize within,* and that means your spouse must come first. When your marriage comes first, everything else falls into its proper place.

I realize this may be a strange idea for many wives and husbands. The hard-driving husband who is out there "breaking his neck for his wife and the kids" working sixty or seventy hours a week may find it just too hard to swallow. And it may seem impossible to a mom with three little ankle-biters who consume her twenty-four hours a day. Just *where* is she supposed to find all this time for her husband (assuming he's even around)?

Nevertheless, I stand by my top priority. For any couple—particularly the overly busy, hard-driving husbands and wives who are trying to juggle career and family—there is more reason than ever to seek refuge in each other, to have some time for yourselves. To keep your family together, you must start at the bottom—at the foundation of it all—your marriage relationship. Finding time for each other can be done—if you both really want to.

Reality Discipline asks the hard questions that help you develop the best priorities.

- What is really important to me? to my spouse? to my children?
- What are our family's goals? What do we want to accomplish in the next ten to fifteen years? the next five years? this year? in the next few months?
- If we take a certain course of action, what will be the consequences for everyone concerned? Does it build the security of every family member, or does it leave someone feeling left out, threatened, or not as important as the others?
- Do we have time for this? If not, are we willing to give up something else in order to make time for this?
- Can we afford this? Is this the best time to buy or invest in something like this? (Possibly most important, "Is this something we need or want?")
- Is this issue or question really worth taking a stand? A key part of using Reality Discipline is to determine what it's worth slugging it out with friend, foe, relative, or family member. What principle is really involved? Am I trying to teach something? live something out that really matters?

All these questions center on the issue of values. What is really important to your entire family? Once you identify your real values, using Reality Discipline becomes much easier. In fact, it becomes second nature.

DON'T FORGET . . .

- To ensure family success, put your spouse first. Beware of the tyranny of the urgent. Make time for the really important. One spouse cannot hold the family together. Both spouses must play an active and equal role.
- Husband or wife, your career should never come ahead of people close to you.
- All you have to invest is your time.
- When choosing priorities, there are four basic disciplines: delaying gratification, accepting responsibility, dedicating yourself to truth, and becoming balanced.

Chapter Five

THE REAL PROBLEM*

Dr. Larry Crabb

In six weeks I would be twenty-two years old. In three weeks I would be a husband. The first I was prepared for; the second, well, that's what I was here for.

I was sitting on an old worn-velvet love seat in the preacher's living room. Nestled close beside me was Rachael, my beautiful bride-to-be. It would have been difficult to slide even a thin book between us.

Across from us, in separate chairs perhaps ten feet apart, sat the preacher and his wife, both in their late seventies. She nodded her gray head and smiled and listened and rocked as her hands worked a rapid rhythm with yarn and knitting needles. He was relaxed into an old stuffed recliner, busily jotting notes in a small, well-used black notebook.

As we discussed the details of our wedding ceremony, I found myself watching the old couple, not as preacher and preacher's wife, but as husband and wife. Suddenly something struck me. Those two, sitting in separate chairs with more than three yards between them, conveyed more love with a single meeting of their eyes than my fiancée and I were exchanging with all our snuggling, grinning, and whispered endearments.

I still remember thinking, *How do we get from here to there, from where we are in our eager young love to where they are in their loving maturity?*

*Adapted from *Men & Women: Enjoying the Difference* by Dr. Larry Crabb. Copyright © 1991 by Lawrence J. Crabb, Jr. Used by permission.

Marriage is a stage on which real love—the kind the apostle Paul described as the greatest virtue—can be enacted for the world to see: the kind of love that enables us to endure wrong with patience, to resist evil with conviction, to enjoy the good things with gusto, to give richly of ourselves with humility, and to nourish another's soul with long-suffering.

When all these virtues are present, not only is each marriage partner incomparably blessed, but sometimes a couple of young apprentices about to take their place on this same stage can catch a glimpse of what the marriage relationship could be—a glimpse that won't let them settle for anything less.

But wanting is one thing; becoming is quite another.

WHAT GETS IN THE WAY?

Why are so few on the path to enjoying the kind of love the preacher and his wife could share from ten feet apart?

Most of us want to be more loving and patient, but it feels as if we're struggling against a power pulling us in the opposite direction. And, like quicksand, that power usually wins. Something has hold of us that won't let go.

I suggest that freeing ourselves to express all that we can be sometimes leads us not to intimacy but to arrogant independence. And efforts to do right without understanding how deeply selfishness taints our motives leads us not to closeness but to stiff courtesy.

Neither the egalitarian nor the traditional model for understanding biblical marriage strongly enough exposes self-centeredness as our basic problem. The egalitarian's replacing of a hierarchical arrangement with a relationship of mutual freedom could foster an unhealthy interest in developing and freeing oneself, thereby strengthening self-centeredness. The traditionalist's attention to gender-specific roles could encourage a moralistic obedience that hides self-centered purposes behind good behavior.

We need to cut through the debate about headship and submission to expose clearly the insidious and pervasive commitment to ourselves that violates love. Once self-centeredness is recognized as the real culprit and other-centeredness as the highest ideal, then we can ask whether an other-centered marriage will reflect egalitarian freedom or hierarchical order.

First, though, we must focus on the real problem: self-centeredness. And nothing brings self-centeredness more clearly into focus than anger.

THE EXPERIENCE OF ANGER

Everyone knows what it's like to be angry with someone. And when we're angry, we're not really concerned with the welfare of the person we're mad at. Anger, at least the kind we're familiar with, is incompatible with love.

But two observations about the experience of anger often escape our notice. First, *we can be angry and not know it.* Parents are sometimes deeply resentful of their children, but they hide their resentment behind displays of excessive warmth and disciplined reasonableness. An unplanned child, for example, can cause a parent to struggle terribly with bitterness; this may give way to guilt over the bitterness that only suppression can handle. Even planned and fully welcome children, when they don't live up to expectations, can provoke disappointment and anger that parents often mask with strong but insincere declarations of "We love you just as you are." Anger can be present but denied.

The second thing about anger we sometimes fail to notice is that, with frightening ease, *we assume that our anger is justified.* Without thinking it through, we see our anger as reasonable, natural, warranted by what's happened, and therefore quite acceptable.

Even rage that wishes another harm, the kind of anger good Christians rarely admit to, can seem appropriate.

I was counseling Dennis, a top-level executive with a consulting company. Dennis told me how troubled he was by the strain in his marriage. He and his wife, Marcia, rarely showed affection to each other anymore. Much of the time, Marcia seemed angry and sullen. Dennis was eager to do all he could to relieve the tensions.

In an early session Dennis mentioned in passing a recurrent, puzzling dream. In the dream Marcia, who is perfectly healthy in real life, lay dying of cancer. He was kneeling by her bedside, doing everything in his power to provide comfort. But she wouldn't look at him. She continued to stare at the ceiling, unresponsive to his tearful expressions of love. Dennis had dreamed this dream perhaps a dozen times over the past several years.

A number of sessions later Dennis revealed how Marcia was letting both her body and mind go. She had gained thirty pounds since they married, and she smoked cigarettes and talked on the telephone much of the day. It gradually became clear that he, a professionally up-to-date executive and a regular at the health club, saw Marcia as a fat, boring, undisciplined partner with whom he was stuck for the rest of his life. Because he was a Christian and did not believe in divorce, only her death could provide an acceptable exit from his bondage.

But rather than facing his anger at her and the self-centered approach to life that nourished it, Dennis continued believing he was a patient man doing his best under the circumstances. Pretending patience rather than acknowledging anger preserved his favorable estimate of himself. But his dream had betrayed him.

After reflecting on the dream and looking more honestly at himself, he looked up intently one day and abruptly said, "I really hate her." Now he was angry, and he knew it.

But his next sentence was not, "Oh, wretched man that I am! How shall I escape judgment for hating my wife, the one woman in all the world I promised to love?" What he did say was this: "She wasn't careless at all when I met her. She was concerned with her appearance, had a really nice figure, and liked to read and talk about interesting things. I really can't figure out what's happened to her."

He seemed no more bothered by his hatred toward his wife than a friend of mine felt about his impatience with a mechanic over a car that wouldn't start. For both men, blaming someone other than themselves seemed the natural thing to do.

"YOU MAKE ME ANGRY!"

When we admit to feeling angry, we automatically justify it, as did Dennis, by interpreting other people's actions as adequate cause. Dennis felt he had a right to be angry because Marcia had put on weight and put off reading. Explaining anger by locating its root outside of ourselves is as instinctive as gasping for air when an oxygen supply is cut off. Accepting blame suffocates; shifting blame allows easy breathing. So we shift blame naturally, without effort or thought.

Anger is too revealing an emotion, however, to handle by either *denying its extent* or *finding its cause in someone else,* the two natural ways to deal with it. Anger tells us something about ourselves that deserves attention, something that will need to be exposed and changed before we can move along the path to mature love. To see clearly what keeps us from getting along, look more closely at what happens in us when we are angry.

LOOKING BENEATH OUR ANGER

A quick peek beneath the surface of anger is enough to see that much of the rage we feel when something bad happens to us grows out of self-centeredness. When we become angry, we become less concerned with other people's welfare and more protective of our own.

If left to develop, this diminished concern for the people we're angry with can progress to the point where we may actually relish the thought of their being hurt. From there, it isn't a giant step to so twist our understanding of justice that we come to believe something bad *should* befall them.

We may not hope a car hits them or they lose their job (though thoughts like that do sometimes cross our minds), but we often feel strangely satisfied with the suffering they endure because of our selfish treatment of them. After all, it's what they deserve for how they have wronged us.

Alex and Jane came to me for counseling. Jane had had an affair four years earlier. She repented, begged Alex to accept her back, and worked hard at becoming a supportive, responsive wife.

In my first session with them, Jane said, "It seems that the harder I try to satisfy him, the nastier he gets. I can only handle it for so long. When I fall apart, Alex seems content for a while and lets me alone. But when I start feeling pretty good again, the verbal abuse picks up until he gets me in tears. I'm really tired of this cycle."

Alex sat there, unmoved by Jane's distress. When I asked him how he was feeling, he answered, "It's hard to understand why she should be treated well after all she's done."

When we're this angry, when we feel as Alex did toward his wife, we feel like God is on our side. We join God (really replace him) in meting out retribution. But even worse, our indignation over the sins of others blinds us to all sense of personal fault. Alex was not seeing how his focus on himself was contributing to his marital problems. In this condition, we deny ourselves the joys of grace and live as natural men and women, incapable of meaningful love.

Most of us, however, don't let things slide to that degree. We deal with anger more quickly and directly. We check its expression, we forgive, and we behave in a civil and sometimes actually kind fashion, often immediately congratulating ourselves for our "good behavior."

Moral efforts such as these may not lessen anger; more often, they merely cover it with a blanket of courtesy containing only a few rips through which our anger leaks out in small doses—little doses that divert personal energy toward ourselves and away from others.

Think how commonly this occurs among "good" people. Reflect on the past few weeks. Remember when you felt annoyed with your spouse, perhaps only mildly and momentarily. Notice what you did or said that was intended to cause pain or get even or keep someone safely under control. Remember when you

- reminded your husband during dinner with friends that the pecan pie was not on his cholesterol-lowering diet?
- cast your wife a withering glance for the stupid comment she just made in the Bible study?
- corrected, with a lightly superior tone, your husband's error in reporting to friends the date of last year's vacation?
- heard your wife start a sentence just as you began reading your favorite newspaper column, consciously tuned her out, and then, a few moments later, irritably asked, "What did you say?"
- sat still when you heard the garage door open, knowing that your wife was arriving home with a carful of groceries, then got up only when she stumbled through the door with two overflowing bags and angrily called out, "Are you going to just sit there? I've got six more bags in the trunk."

During each of these interactions, devotion to the partner's happiness was edged out in favor of stronger concern for oneself. In each case, self-centered energy was flowing, fueling anger and directing its expression.

And the anger, as we've already seen, is hard to admit but easy to excuse. Why is something that gets in the way of loving our mate so difficult to recognize? And, more important, why does our anger, and the selfish, hurtful things we do when we're angry, so often seem reasonable and so rarely make us feel truly guilty?

Resentful thoughts should provoke guilt, but more often we regard our bitterness, not as the product of a flaw within us, but as the interplay between our delicate sensitivities and other people's failures. We think others should be rebuked while our damaged souls receive healing. Why is it so hard to see that self-interest, even when offended, is wrong, so wrong that, in fact, we deserve not kindly treatment but the harshest possible judgment?

Some would argue that there's nothing to feel guilty about, at least not when we get angry and stand up for ourselves. When a wife admits to an affair, as Jane did, her husband understandably feels hurt and angry. In most cases, during the period of reconciliation, he needs to tell her honestly how he feels. And a concern to avoid further hurt is completely normal. But when Alex's attitude reflects *no higher priority* than expressing himself and recovering from the blow, then perhaps he is wrongly self-centered.

Others suggest that our anger is really holy anger against sin, the same kind God feels. Maybe we really are right in getting angry with our spouse: "She never supports me when I discipline the kids." "I hate going shopping with him. He always turns his head to look at pretty women." Maybe we are legitimately angry because our spouse is clearly wrong.

But that answer won't do. Calling our anger righteous is a high claim. God's anger never violates his perfect character of holiness and love. In his anger he never perverts justice; he never takes sadistic pleasure in seeing someone suffer, even when it is deserved; and he never compromises or reduces his commitment to people's well-being.

The anger we're more familiar with, the natural and bad kind, points up a fault in our characters that simply isn't there in God's, a fault that interferes with our getting along with one another.

THE BASIC FLAW

Anger isn't the core issue; nor is the pretense that it doesn't exist. The diminished concern for others that always accompanies anger moves us closer to the central flaw but doesn't get us quite all the way. And it's not adequate to describe the basic flaw in our character merely as self-centeredness. Certainly this comes close.

Careful inspection of ourselves, particularly when we're angry, makes it clear that we suffer from a defect more severe than mere self-centeredness. The greatest obstacle to building truly good relationships is *justified* self-centeredness, a selfishness that, deep in our souls, feels entirely reasonable and therefore acceptable in light of how we've been treated.

The apostle Paul, I think, held a similar notion. Before moving into a clear presentation of the gospel of Christ in his letter to the Romans, Paul spends nearly three chapters clearing away all excuses for sin. When every mouth is stopped and people are utterly unable to justify their sinful, selfish ways before God, *then* Paul introduces the wonder of God's grace. The gospel cannot be enjoyed until all excuses for sin are removed. And the fruit of the gospel—getting along with God and with one another—will develop to the degree that we recognize self-centeredness, see it as inexcusably wrong, and repent of it.

We do, however, have a hard time seeing ourselves as all that guilty. When we confess our faults to God or to one another, we usually try to *explain away* our sin. "You're right. I shouldn't have done that. I was wrong. I'll do my best to not do that again. If only my wife were more supportive, I think I'd have a better chance of licking this problem."

Explanations are requests not for *forgiveness* but for *understanding*. When we regard our wrong actions as understandable, we feel only a little guilty. But meaningful repentance and enduring change require more than casual confession of guilt. And they also require more than others strongly denouncing our selfishness and firmly exhorting us to selflessness. Movement from self-centeredness toward other-centeredness happens only when we expose our excuses for selfishness and regard those excuses as entirely illegitimate.

But this is not easily done. Whether our sins are big evils, like adultery, spouse-beating, and alcoholism, or lesser ones like impatience, overeating, and gossip, the inclination to excuse ourselves, to see ourselves as right, is terribly strong.

A friend of mine confessed to me that he had committed adultery. He later told me his wife was so unsupportive of the tensions he lived with every day that his desire to be appreciated by a woman simply got the best of him. "And," he added, "when I explain all of that to my wife, she just doesn't understand. I've decided to do the right thing and stick with my wife, but let me tell you, it's hard. It would sure help if she understood me better."

Adulterers often have a distorted perspective on how life works. They see their sin as necessary to their soul's well-being and therefore more understandable than wrong. And a powerful urge more basic than lust—the wish to be understood and appreciated by a member of the opposite sex—carries them along a path that seems inevitable. Whatever voice of conscience remains gets swept away like a stick in a tidal wave.

Those of us not guilty of the more heinous sins shake our heads in disbelief that anyone could ever rationalize such obvious evil. We are proudly unaware that the same mechanism for excusing sin operates regularly within us, rendering us vulnerable to the worst sins imaginable.

A simple illustration will make this point clear. A husband arrives home an hour late, detained at the office by pressing deadlines. As he walks through the door, his wife, without bothering to get up from the couch, greets him flatly: "Your meal is on a plate in the micro. You can heat it up if you want."

Immediately he feels defensive, considers explaining his late arrival, then thinks better of it (*What's the use? She's too irritated to listen*). Without saying a word, he walks past her to the bedroom. As he takes off his tie and splashes his face with water, he rehearses an attack on her for her unsupportive attitude, decides to skip it (*it would only cause more hassle*) and just go eat.

It doesn't occur to him that *she* may be feeling neglected and insensitively treated. If it had, the thought of gently moving toward her would feel too risky and weak, certainly uncalled-for at that moment.

He therefore returns to the kitchen, pushes the appropriate buttons on the microwave oven, and stares at his meal through the glass door until the bell sounds. As he carries his plate to the now deserted dinner table, he feels angry satisfaction in meeting her irritability with his noiseless sulk. "Does she really think I *enjoy* working late?" he mutters to himself.

As he plunges his knife into the barely warm meal, his mind drifts to last weekend's shopping trip when *she* bought a dress and *he* passed up the sport coat he had been wanting for months.

As he continues eating, the pleasure generated by his angry thoughts fades; loneliness arrives in its place. He realizes that he could have called to say he would be home later than expected. He decides to make things right with his wife.

He walks to the living room, sits down next to her, and, speaking loudly enough to be heard over the television, apologizes for being late. He gently explains his lateness, showing an understanding of his wife's mood.

She softens under the influence of his tender spirit and, with mutual promises to be more thoughtful of one another, they unite in a hug that begins a pleasant evening.

The harmony thereby restored is not solid. The promises are not strong. As I have described this event, it's clear that the husband apologized to relieve his own loneliness rather than to soothe his wife's hurt. Like most apologies, his included an explanation for the offense, making it into a request for understanding. His was not a true apology.

True apologies never explain, they only admit, acknowledging that the error was without justifiable cause. Repentant people realize that inexcusable wrong can either be judged or forgiven, never understood and overlooked, and so they beg for forgiveness with no thought of deserving it. Truly repentant people are the ones who begin to grasp God's amazing grace, the ones who know that they need only confess to experience the forgiveness that is always there in infinite supply.

Whether we are adulterers or thoughtless spouses, the problem with all of us is that we stubbornly regard our interpersonal failures not as *inexcusably selfish choices* but as *understandable mistakes*. The things our spouses do to us seem more like the former; the things we do to them more like the latter.

Excuse-making has been a natural tendency in people ever since Adam blamed Eve and Eve blamed the snake. Without some means of self-justification, we would be forced to face ourselves squarely as we really are, corrupt by God's standards and deserving punishment.

And seeing ourselves as we are would mean taking our place as condemned sinners, worthy of judgment, powerless to improve ourselves, humbled that our very best deeds provide no defense, and utterly at the mercy of a righteously angry judge. This doesn't sound like much fun. Surely the path to the top would never begin with a descent *this* steep! How can joy emerge from such misery?

Perhaps the hardest thing to get through our brain-damaged heads (when Adam fell, he must have fallen on his head) is that this painful point of nakedness and humility is not only where life begins but also where joyful growth continues.

More than anything else, what gets in the way of getting along is self-centeredness that seems reasonable. God does his deepest work in making us more truly loving when we more clearly see how utterly ugly our selfishness is.

Getting along with each other requires that we stop making excuses for all the selfish things we do. And if our tendency toward self-justification can be weakened, perhaps then we will more easily recognize our anger when it's there, call it wrong, and experience the thrill of Christ's forgiveness and the power of his cleansing. We're not condemned, and we're empowered to love.

Weakening this inclination to self-justification is hard work. Not many undertake it. But it is possible to change. The next chapter tells you how.

Chapter Six

CHANGE IS POSSIBLE*

Dr. Larry Crabb

Okay, I'm selfish. So what else is new?" We tend to view self-centeredness the way we look at eating a second dessert: It may not be right, but it isn't that big a problem. Most of us are occupied with other, much more serious problems—controlling our sexual appetites, coping with loneliness, trying to get along with family and colleagues, making financial ends meet, keeping ourselves in decent health. Selfishness just doesn't feel like a major concern. But it is!

Unless we are struck with the inexcusable wrongness and the deadly power of self-centeredness, we will not make much progress in becoming other-centered. We will overlook the selfish motives rumbling beneath much of what we do, and we will dismiss as acceptable error whatever selfishness we do own: "Well, yes, it is terribly wrong to think only of oneself. We mustn't do that."

Times when we are struck with the sheer evil of self-centeredness cannot be arranged. Most often, they come at surprising times and deliver unexpected impact. One of those moments seized me during a casual conversation.

I was sitting in an outdoor cafe in Capetown, enjoying coffee and conversation with British theologian D. Broughton Knox. Around us bustled the life of the beautiful South African city. Rising behind us was the awesome backdrop of cold mountains, shooting up proudly and then disappearing indifferently into

---

*Adapted from *Men & Women: Enjoying the Difference* by Dr. Larry Crabb. Copyright © 1991 by Lawrence J. Crabb, Jr. Used by permission.

white clouds. To one side, open fields stretched for acres, blooming with nature's patchwork quilt of wildflowers.

A comfortable pause in our conversation allowed the surrounding beauty to put me in a pensive mood. Finally I broke the silence by posing to my companion what I thought was a complex and thoughtful question, the kind that lesser minds wrangle over for generations.

"Why is it, do you suppose, that people have such a hard time getting along with each other?"

Dr. Knox is well known for his brilliant mind and is even seen by some as rather formidable. Challenging his views is risky business, for he never adopts a position without carefully thinking through the alternatives. He's also able to express important ideas in simple words because he understands those ideas so well.

As I spoke he watched me with flattering attention. Then, with neither arrogance nor hesitation, he said, "Well, the whole thing comes down to selfishness, doesn't it? Isn't it interesting how people complicate it all so much? I suppose we don't like seeing ourselves as we really are."

The fresh clarity and strong impact of his words staggered me. What enormous implications they held: All our relationship problems spring from one place—the foul well of selfishness!

If this is true, I thought, then the real problem we must tackle is to understand how self-centered people can become other-centered people.

Since then, however, I have realized that we must work on another problem first. It rarely has impact to be told that we are really selfish. Many of us readily plead guilty to the charge. Privately, of course, we think the crime is not terribly serious. A misdemeanor perhaps, worthy of a small fine.

Our first job, then, is to attack head-on this reliable habit of thinking that our selfishness is understandable in light of the struggles we face and that more serious concerns require our attention. We must see that fitting into prescribed roles or freeing ourselves from oppression are not the most important things we can do to learn to get along with one another as God intended. These are lower priorities than repenting of self-centeredness.

Every effort we make to restore people to godly functioning must deal with the problem of justified selfishness. Efforts that focus on something else—whether bludgeoning people into conformity through confrontation, or liberating them psychologically through therapy and socially through asserting rights—badly miss the point.

Personal diagnosis is always unpleasant for sinful people. Honest self-evaluation reliably leads to unflattering observations about ourselves. But diagnosis, no matter how deflating, must precede treatment, because it informs us what treatment is needed and makes us gratefully willing to receive it.

What will it take to convince us that our selfishness is without excuse and that our first job, in our friendships and marriages, is to recognize our selfishness and learn how we can change?

To answer this question, we need to grasp three things: our greatest need is forgiveness, only God's law has the power to shatter our excuses, and change occurs only in the context of hope.

OUR GREATEST NEED IS FORGIVENESS

In John Bunyan's classic allegory *Pilgrim's Progress,* Pilgrim, the main character, begins his journey weighted down by a heavy burden strapped tightly to his back. Like a severe toothache, this load fully consumes his attention. Nothing matters more to him than getting free of it.

The intolerable weight represents Pilgrim's sin, and he cannot gain relief from it until, after climbing a hill, he finds forgiveness waiting for him at the cross. Pilgrim then becomes Christian and sets off in single-minded pursuit of the Celestial City.

If we were to rewrite *Pilgrim's Progress* today, reflecting values prevailing in many of our Christian communities, Pilgrim might be renamed Victim, and his burden, rather than sin symbolized by a backbreaking weight, might become a tightly bound soul gasping for air. Or perhaps the burden would be an injured soul, represented by an open wound on his body, inflicted by friends who, with neither cause nor warning, turned on him and used him cruelly for their own advantage.

If the writer of this updated version were a moralist, release from Victim's confinement and recovery from his wound would no doubt come through stern admonishments to obey God, duly heeded by a chastened Victim who, after enough time had elapsed to demonstrate a consistent pattern of moral living, would be called Pharisee.

But poor sales, especially among the growing ranks of free thinkers who despise the restrictions of an authority outside themselves, might quickly lead to a second edition, this one written by someone who understands the thoroughly human cry for freedom.

In this even more updated version (and this one likely would break all sales records), Victim becomes Himself or Herself (or, to avoid any hint of sexism, Itself) and learns to break free from all dependency in relationships and to live a self-affirmed, creatively alive, independent existence. The story ends when Himself or Herself reaches the Kingdom of Self and lives in utopian harmony with other selves, each one committed entirely to his or her own freedom.[1]

In each new edition, the difficulty is less with the proposed solution and more with the diagnosed problem. Each author has shifted from identifying the burden as *sin* to seeing it as *restriction* or as a personal *wound.*

The moralistic author whose hero became Pharisee would quickly insist with pharisaical indignation that he has not, of course, made that shift. The problem, in his eyes, continues to be sin that must be confronted and abandoned.

But to the degree that his exhortations to holy living are a response to Victim's cry for understanding and help, the moralist has shifted away from a biblical view of sin. Victim's cry for help needs to be heard. He is wounded, injured by the mistreatment of others. His pain needs to be understood, not dismissed with a scolding. *But the use made of this pain—justifying self-centered living—must be exposed and condemned.*

Responding to people's pain with an exhortation to live properly sometimes reflects an uncaring heart and a shallow view of sin. People who deeply care and who richly understand sin as more than wrong actions will compassionately but relentlessly expose the problem in such a way that forgiveness, not moral commitment, is seen as the necessary beginning of a solution.

The tendency in modern Christianity is to recommend either *external morality* or *self-development* as the path to abundant living. And we thereby miss the point altogether.

Until we see self-centeredness as the core obstacle in the way of mature Christian living that neither moralistic effort nor personal growth can remove, we will continue to devote our energies to solving lesser problems. Rather than coming to understand how God can in fact change us into more other-centered people by first forgiving our selfishness and thus promoting a deep joy that can survive any crisis, we worry more about changing the painful things in our lives.

WHAT WOULD MAKE US TRULY HAPPY?

It would be an interesting exercise to ask a group of Christian people to write down what they think they need right now, more than anything else, to make them truly happy.

Some, I suspect, would put at the top of their list a closer walk with the Lord. A majority of these, I further suspect, would have on their minds more consistency in spiritual disciplines such as Bible study and prayer. Others would write down social justice in the church and at home. Still others, I think the majority, would turn to the painful struggles in their immediate circumstances and record needs such as these:

- a husband who would stop drinking
- a more sexually interested wife
- a medical report that the tissue is benign
- a better job
- more money
- a man to marry
- an estranged son coming home
- a rebellious daughter straightening out
- a husband or wife or parent or child coming to Christ

These concerns are deeply felt, both in the hearts of the list-makers and in the heart of God. And each one brings pain into our lives that won't go away until someone else or something outside of ourselves changes. It is right and good to pray fervently that God would make the change we desire.

But each of these responses is a wrong answer to the question, What do I need *more than anything else* to make me deeply happy? There is only one correct answer: forgiveness from God that brings me into relationship with him and ongoing forgiveness that makes continued fellowship possible. Every other answer is wrong.

If we had asked, *Other* than forgiveness, what do I need right now to make me happy? then many of the above answers could be quite correct. We tend, however, to define our problems, at least our currently most pressing ones, in such a way that something other than forgiveness is seen as our greatest need. But this tendency reflects our darkened understanding of life.

Without the power of forgiveness operating in my life right now, even as I write this sentence, I remain alone and unloved, uncared for by anyone who is fully committed to my well-being, locked into an existence with no point, "tired of living and scared of dying," capable of enjoying only those pleasures that mask reality and afterward increase my sense of emptiness, and afraid to face the awful freedom of choosing my way in the dark.

Somehow, and it is a tribute to the ingenuity of devilish wisdom, we manage to believe that we do not really need continued forgiveness. We may give forgiveness its preeminent place in public confession, but privately we're quite persuaded that something else is really more vital to our lives. Forgiveness seems more important as a once laid foundation for our lives than as a presently and continually needed reality. Forgiveness *begins* the Christian life, but, we assume, something else (moral effort? self-development?) sustains it. And whatever it is, we pursue it with evangelistic fervor and thus continue on in an essentially self-centered approach to life.

Relationship with God established *and maintained* by his forgiveness provides the only framework within which we can be concerned with our own well-being without being wrongly self-centered. And this is because entering into that relationship and learning to enjoy it more deeply requires that we depend not on our own efforts to gain life or to protect ourselves from pain but rather on whatever a kind God chooses to do as we repentantly follow him. John Piper, in *Desiring God,* describes a similar idea that he calls Christian hedonism and rightly commends it.

When we move from an indifference about our selfishness to a convicting awareness of it, an awareness that makes forgiveness more important to us right now than anything else we can imagine, then we are on the road to building good relationships. But how do we make that move?

ONLY GOD'S LAW CAN SHATTER OUR EXCUSES

People hurt. All of us do. We were designed to live in a far better world than the one we now inhabit. In the better world yet ahead for God's family, we will care deeply about one another. Complaining will be as foreign to our purified natures as disease to our then perfect bodies.

In this world, things are not that way. We are lonely. We are wounded by rejection, angered by cruelty, disillusioned by power-hungry Christian leaders, exhausted by endless responsibilities, saddened by distance from loved ones, confused and hurt by family tensions, grieved beyond words by the suffering of a terminally ill child, and troubled to the point of breakdown by upsetting changes in our lives.

Both the godly and the ungodly seem to enjoy the opportunities of life, despite its trials. Godly people joyfully delight in good things—a tasty meal, a weekend away, the company of friends—and nobly endure hard things—an anorexic daughter, a layoff, betrayal by a friend. They know that their existence is meaningful and that they are destined for unlimited pleasure at the deepest level. Because they keenly feel that nothing now quite meets the standards of their longing souls, the quiet but deeply throbbing ache within them drives them not to complaint but to anticipation and further yieldedness.

The difference between godly and ungodly people is not that one group never hurts and the other group does, or that one reports more happiness than the other. The difference lies in what people do with their hurt. Either they do what comes naturally—use their hurt to justify self-centered efforts to relieve it, caring less about how they affect others and more about whether they are comfortable—or they do what comes unnaturally—use their hurt to better understand and encourage others while they cling desperately to the Lord for promised deliverance, passionately determined to do his will.[2]

The best of us sometimes yield to the tendency to justify a consuming interest in ourselves. Our thoughts run along these lines:

- Anyone who knew what I've endured and how hard I work to just keep my head above water, and how bad I sometimes feel, would take a noncritical interest in me and try to help. My situation really does justify my thinking more about how I'm making it than worrying about you and your problems.

- When we're together, I feel hurt when you don't ask many questions about how things are going for me. Well, yes, I don't ask much about you, that's true, and I'm sure I should be more interested in you, but I've had such a time with my kids. One of mine is still home all day, you know; yours are all in school, aren't they?

- And did you know our newer car (it's three years old) is in for repairs again? By the way, I do like the new one you're driving. And the carpet man said he couldn't install our new carpets for two more weeks. It's just one thing after the other.

- Oh, did I tell you that we're not going to be able to get away for Christmas and my parents aren't able to come here either? Sometimes I wonder if my kids even know they have grandparents . . .

We are so easily caught up in ourselves. It comes so naturally. When we prattle on about our lives in a mood of "I've got it harder than anybody else," no one really listens, and all but the most seasoned prattlers sense that any display of interest from others is at best polite.

We end these doleful conversations feeling uncared for, believing that our friends are selfishly insensitive. The thought of reaching out to *them* seems unbearable; they should come to us to prove their friendship.

Justified self-centeredness is such an automatic and well-practiced premise for our thinking about relationships that only the hammer of God's law can break it apart. And it does so in an unexpected way.

Most of us would prefer to think of God warmly cheering us on as we try to keep our balance in the storms of life. And God does deeply encourage. But something in our character brings out another part of his, making him less the cheerleader rooting us to victory and more the determined surgeon wielding a knife.

He sees in us what we, with eyes marred by convenient blind spots, fail to recognize. We think our deepest struggles are coping with a disagreeable spouse or finding a snatch of comfort in a terribly uncomfortable world. But God sees the cancer of self-centeredness that has tainted our most patient and heroic deeds. In keeping with his relentless concern for our perfect health, he hangs copies of the alarming x-rays all about our room, intending to make us aware of our desperate condition.

But we look away, governed by the mistaken idea that someone who understood our hurt would respond with only sympathy and support. Meanwhile, God, who understands even those hurts that we've forgotten, continues to discourage us with reminders of our failure to love perfectly, refusing to bend even an inch in his demand for perfection.

The law of God is relentlessly rigid. It never gives anyone a break because no one, regardless of what he or she has suffered, *deserves* a break. Total other-centeredness is required of us at every moment, whether in the presence of a caring friend or an unfaithful spouse. The slightest compromise with purity ends any hope of acceptance by God. People who present the quality of their lives to God as grounds for relationship with him will instead be removed from his presence.

Creatures like us, who are so prone to excusing our lack of love for others by reminding ourselves how poorly others love us, need to see that God, even when we hurt the most, commands us to respond with unstained love.

But he doesn't *expect* us to; in fact, he knows that we won't. His inflexible commandments are intended to acquaint us with another dimension of his character: his grace, a dimension only those who have failed and admitted it can enjoy.

Our choice, then, once we admit we cannot do all that we're told to do, becomes *either* to call the law bad (and to prepare our defense for the day when we're summoned to the eternal court by listing every injury that we've sustained from life) or to admit that it is we who are bad.

Now, admitting we're bad is quite another matter from despising who we are. Many of us vaguely sense that we are not quite what we should be. But often, this discomfort is an illegitimate disdain for ourselves that developed when imperfect authorities in our lives used impossible standards of behavior to reject us.

It is thoroughly proper to desire escape from the dark night of mean-spirited rejection into the brightness of God's accepting grace. But often the route of escape takes us first through an even darker night, where we stand alone before a fair judge, forced to admit that his anger toward us is a deserved response to our real failure.

THE PROPER ATTITUDE: HUMBLE CONFESSION

The ongoing attitude of the maturing, self-aware Christian is one of humble confession: "Lord, at every moment of my life, regardless of the hurt I experience, your law condemns me. Your standards are right, but I cannot meet them. I am not good enough to do what you require. I am worthy of judgment. Forgiveness is my deepest need right now and will continue to be my deepest need till I die. Because your atoning death meets that need, I can live in the freedom of forgiveness, neither obsessed with my sin nor indifferent toward it."

God could randomly select any five-minute slice from our lives and, after evaluating our thoughts, motives, and deeds during this brief period, *justly* throw us into outer darkness to wander forever alone in agony and despair. When we begin to grasp this, our excuses appear weak and our selfishness deadly. We are then on our way to enjoying grace and to becoming more other-centered.

When we hear the demands of the law repeated with firm insistence during even our hardest times, our excuses for self-centeredness are shattered. We can *then* hear the whispers of his love: "You're forgiven. Everything's okay. Enjoy!" Not our efforts to be more loving but God's forgiveness is the foundation for everything good that we bring to our relationships.

Perhaps a simple example will make the point.

A husband and wife are wandering the aisles of a grocery store together, she in the lead, he pushing the cart behind her. He did not want to come, but his wife (for reasons unclear to him) expressed a strong desire for his company. So, feeling noble, he agreed to come.

Stopping in front of a large display of spices, the wife methodically scans each row. Cumin, coriander, cloves, cream of tartar. He wonders why the search is taking so long and asks, with poorly concealed impatience, "What are you looking for?" She inarticulately mutters the name of a spice he would not recognize if clearly pronounced.

He feels a sudden surge of irritability. "What do you need it for anyway? I'm really getting hungry."

Throwing him a withering look of disbelief, she snaps back, "I don't know why I asked you to come," and tears off down the aisle, hurt and angry.

Suppose, just after the spice was incoherently pronounced and the husband first became aware of his impatience, he had thought to himself, *I'm really annoyed that she's taking more time than seems necessary to look for one special spice. I know I'm feeling a bit noble for agreeing to come; I was tired after a long day at work. I feel that she really ought to be sensitive to my fatigue and appreciative that I came and, therefore, move faster. I'm asking her to look out for me.*

But God wants me to use this opportunity to somehow encourage her.
Anything less than a genuine desire to bless her (and actions consis-
tent with this purpose) deserves judgment.

THREE POSSIBLE RESPONSES

If the husband thought along these lines, he might react in
one of three ways. He might feel *enraged* that God would require
him to be kind to her when he has already done more than his
share of good deeds. *It's not fair that I be required to look out for her*
right now. It's my turn to be kindly treated. He then might poke her
with the cart to move her along. The apostle Paul spoke of God's
law arousing our sinful passions (see Romans 7:5).

Second, he might *commit himself to do better.* Rather than
admitting that he simply is not capable of loving her in that
moment (or any other) with the perfect love God requires, he
determines to treat her well. But when he realizes that God
requires him to treat her *perfectly* from a thoroughly willing heart
controlled completely by love for her, then he despairs. He already
broke his commitment when his selfish heart became irritated
over a moment of inconvenience. The only way to keep his commitment is to lower God's standards to a level he can meet. And
then, if he meets them, he will become proud.

There is a third possible response: He might admit his inability to do what is right, be shamed by his tendency to excuse an
unkind reaction to his wife, and *plead for mercy.* This is the only
one of the three choices that will lead the husband to other-
centeredness. God gives standards, not first of all to teach us how
to live, but to convince us that we can't meet them. We simply
aren't good enough. It isn't only that we're weak. We are *selfish,*
more interested in ourselves than anyone else. The third choice
puts the husband in reach of God's transforming grace and makes
possible humble efforts to treat his wife well.

We can stand before God, equipped with all our excuses, and he, fully understanding those excuses, still pronounces us guilty. The vision of this scene must become embedded in our thinking, strengthened by studying what God says in his Word about sin, reinforced by honest feedback from our friends and spouse about the ways in which we act selfishly, and nourished by reflection on these selfish thoughts and feelings and our excuses for them.

The more we realize that our performance, even as mature Christians, will never reach the level of perfection needed to avoid his wrath, the more our excuses for sin will shatter under the weight of fear. And we will enter into a despair that only the kindness of God can relieve.

CHANGE OCCURS IN THE CONTEXT OF HOPE

This may sound strange, but listening to God's law makes it possible, as nothing else does, for me to see the kindness in his heart.

More than two hundred years ago, Jonathan Edwards expressed a similar thought:

> Seek that you may see that you are utterly undone, and that you cannot help yourself, and yet, that you do not deserve that God should help you, and that He would be perfectly just if He should refuse to ever help you. If you have come to this, then you will be prepared for comfort. When persons are thus humble, it is God's manner soon to comfort them.[3]

Removing excuses for sin creates an awareness of our most basic need—forgiveness—but by itself does not draw us to God. If matters are left there, we are in an awful mess.

But understanding how completely we deserve judgment, even for impatience by a spice rack, helps us to see why God delays in administering it. If God's law expresses his character, then surely he is never indifferent to our sin. His delay in meting out justice rather reflects his patience. He does not want anyone to perish, but everyone to repent (see 2 Peter 3:9).

For Christians, those of us who have already trusted Christ for salvation, it is humbling to realize that God's patience makes it possible for us to understand our sin more thoroughly and to learn deeper levels of both repentance and joy.

Take the husband by the spice rack, for example. The man described in the incident was converted to Christ more than thirty-five years ago. I know, because I am he.

I can be confronted with the continuing sinfulness of my heart, realize that my only hope is forgiveness, and then, conscious that where sin abounds, grace abounds even more, begin to sense the welcome movement of God's Spirit, prompting me to deal gently with Rachael, my wife. Now my determination to do right involves a passionate warmth toward Rachael. Obedience becomes less a mechanical choice and more a wanted direction.

It may take years, but facing the requirements of God in a way that shatters our excuses for self-centered living and becoming aware of his forgiveness will lead to surprising evidence of change.

No one turns to someone who condemns. A walk to the courthouse is never pleasant for one whose speeding was accurately registered by radar. But, once condemned, we long to find someone who forgives. Once we understand the extent of God's judgment, our longing for forgiveness becomes literally the most intense desire of our condemned hearts, crowding out all those lesser desires for pleasure, fame, or merely human companionship. Nothing matters more to the person trapped in a burning house than getting out.

The mystery, of course, is that the one who completely condemns is the same one who completely forgives. God is both holy and loving. But we cannot enjoy his love until we are first crushed by the weight of his holiness. To put it another way, we have no interest in his forgiveness until we see our need of it. The more we become aware of how thoroughly self-centered we are, the more important and wonderful his forgiveness becomes.

Proud people have no sense of impending judgment. They expect compliments and thereby never learn of God's forgiving grace. Humble people, however, meet God in all his wonder as an unbending judge whose heart of love has found a way to forgive them and to restore them to relationship with himself.

When we in our sin meet God in his grace—this does the most to change us. And an ongoing encounter with God, in which we further probe the depths of his forgiveness, not by sinning more but by recognizing more of our sin, continues the process of change.

When more than anything else we long for forgiveness, we then learn to celebrate forgiveness as the foundation of our lives. His grace, not our effort, becomes everything. And as we value God's grace more, we change from self-centered people who angrily yearn for relief from hurt to other-centered people who celebrate his forgiveness by longing to know him better and to make him better known. Change is not only possible for, but also promised to, the Christian who believes that God is the rewarder of those who diligently seek him.

The core dynamic behind all change from self-centeredness to other-centeredness is an appreciation of God's grace. Many forces promote change: admitting self-pity and behaving responsibly can lift depression; sorting through issues of control may relieve eating compulsions; talking sensibly to yourself during a crisis can quiet anxiety. But only one force can move us toward that radically other-centered character of Christ: the celebration of forgiveness.

Chapter Seven

NEVER QUIT!*

Becky and Dr. Roger Tirabassi

In our first year of marriage, we wrestled with the usual but unwelcome adjustments to married life. Our roles, responsibilities, and freedoms were challenged. Conflicting thoughts and feelings caused us to continually struggle with each other. Regularly, we fell into our ugly patterns of escalating anger (Becky) and withdrawal (Roger). We wanted desperately to create new patterns and avoid so much fighting, but we seemed stuck.

After an episode where we had hurt each other, we decided to pray and ask God to help us resolve our conflicts in a better way the next time they occurred. During Roger's quiet time, he felt that God gave him an idea: We should hold hands, even hug, the next time we felt a conflict of this degree surface. It took only three hours for us to have the opportunity to try this new idea because Roger did something that irritated me! Thus, when Rog approached me to hug in the heat of the situation, I became doubly irritated. Not only was I mad, but I wasn't in the "hug" mood. Rather, I wanted Roger to know that he had hurt me. So, as was my habit, I didn't use a very loving approach, and I proceeded to blast him with my anger. But he persisted, wanting to test the new idea and hug me.

He said, "Let's hug while we talk!" I was not agreeable to that, so I backed away. He came closer, and I continued to backpedal.

He said, "You have to hug me. Remember our plan?"

---

*Adapted from *How to Live with Them Since You Can't Live Without Them* by Becky and Dr. Roger Tirabassi. Copyright © 1998. Used by permission.

I said, "I don't feel like hugging you. It's your plan. My plan is to be mad at you."

He said, "No, it's God's plan and you agreed to it. You have to hug me!"

As he chased me down the hall, we broke into laughter. In my rush to get away from him, I tripped and fell on the floor, and he dived on top of me! We laughed even harder and then we hugged. By that time, it was hard for me to be angry with Rog. For a while, I forgot what he had done to hurt me so badly and make me so mad. Once I remembered what it was, we took the time to talk it out. In this way Roger and I stayed connected to each other during a heated situation. We encourage you to give this simple method a try in your marriage.

DECIDE TO STAY CONNECTED TO YOUR MATE

Right after we got married—in fact, on our honeymoon—we had a huge argument. Roger felt that I needed to spend more time with him. I thought that I should have the same amount of freedom and independence that I had when I was single. Obviously, our opposing ideas created a problem! It took only three days of marriage for us to realize that we would really have to work through this and many more disagreements to come. We became acutely aware that we had to fight *for* our marriage and use every trick in the book to stay connected to each other.

Through trial and error, and deep commitment to each other, we made three fundamental decisions that helped our relationship grow more secure and intimate. We decided that to stay close to each other we had to do the following:

1. Spend quality and quantity time together!
2. Never quit!
3. Become each other's best friend and biggest encourager!

SPEND QUALITY AND
QUANTITY TIME TOGETHER

Because we met and then married while working in the same organization, we knew something about each other: *Both of us* were inclined to work long, hard hours. Either Roger or I would often stay late and work extra hours to complete a difficult or important project. We were equally susceptible to workaholism if given the right circumstances. The one positive aspect of working in the same organization was that we spent many of our working hours *together*. That was true until I became a mother!

After I gave birth to Jacob, we decided that I would change my employee status from paid staff to volunteer. And very quickly, we saw much less of each other.

We soon realized that we had previously set an unhealthy pattern of working too many hours. (It is not unusual for singles and newlyweds to find themselves in a similar situation.) But now, married and parents, we were being destroyed by that work ethic. I will never forget the day that Roger came home from work after seeing the frustration growing within me, and he said that if I felt his work ever became more important than our marriage, he would change jobs or make the necessary adjustments to reprioritize our lives. I was comforted by his words; I truly believed that he would do whatever he had to do to preserve our marriage.

In year three of our marriage and ministry I felt overwhelmed with the amount of ministry time that consumed our daily lives, and I brought his promise to the table. True to his word, Roger immediately made personal and professional adjustments with the use of his time. They were monumental to me.

1. He agreed to be home *on time rather than late* for dinner. He also scheduled fewer dinner meetings, but more breakfast or lunch meetings.

2. He delegated the club meeting that took him to the east side of Cleveland once a week to a person who lived on that side of town, eliminating a four-hour travel and evening meeting commitment from his weekly schedule. The move also gave a new person the opportunity to exercise leadership gifts.

3. In addition, other time commitments and meetings that he changed or condensed modeled a balanced lifestyle to all who worked for him, showing them, by his actions, that his family was most important to him.

Find the Balance

We worked diligently to find the proper balance between family and work during our first twelve years of marriage, regularly evaluating our jobs and lives, until we came to a new juncture when our son, Jake, went into the sixth grade. At that time, Roger worked for a large church. Due to a number of circumstances, his job began to require much more evening and weekend time away from home. We knew that Jake's entering junior high school would entail a whole new set of time commitments. During that period, I was being asked to speak out of town more frequently. It was a turning point for our family.

That time, Roger brought up our need for a lifestyle revision. He felt as if we were a family spinning out of control and not feeling or staying connected. We all admitted that we were barely holding on. Roger feared that Jake would get shortchanged by having two parents with hectic schedules, and he also was concerned that he and I might start to live two separate lives.

He did something very unusual, even radical, for a man with a doctorate and two master's degrees! He suggested that he resign from his full-time position and work part-time in order to free me to pursue my call and dreams, but allow us still to have a parent at home after school. For Roger, that meant a significant salary reduction. But the same decision allowed me to say yes to the groups calling me to speak! And Jake had a new at-home parent— Dad!

Consider the Cost

Before we made the transition, Roger had to consider the cost of my occasional absence. My traveling meant that some of his regular duties would include cooking, doing laundry, grocery shopping, helping with homework, and carpooling! (Mind you, he is an *Italian-raised* man!) It was a touching offer that signaled a departure from the traditional roles of married men and women. But because it was his idea, it gave me a huge vote of his confidence that it was now God's timing to fulfill my call as a writer and speaker.

Since then, Roger has worked in two different part-time positions. In 1994, he founded Spiritual Growth Ministries, and he opened his own pastoral counseling office one mile from our house. (If I might say so myself, he is a most wonderful and gifted pastoral counselor.)

In 1991, I began to speak and write, traveling during the school year, but staying home during the summers and for school vacations during our son's junior high and high school years! The decision to limit my speaking primarily to the school year calendar and to one overnight per trip has allowed our family to spend a great deal of time together. In fact, Roger and I have found that we have stayed *more* connected in our current roles than when we maintained more traditional roles. We talk and pray by telephone each night that I am out of town, and when I get home, we always have a date planned to go to a movie or out to dinner alone or with other couples. And because I travel often, we have accrued travel miles that provide a yearly family vacation with other families we have met through my speaking engagements, widening our circle of friends!

If You Paid the Price, You'll Reap the Blessings!

Seven years with this schedule have gone by and Jake is off in college! We feel that the decisions we made at the different seasons and junctures in our lives to protect our family time and dating life from the urgency and lure of workaholism have allowed us to stay connected, maintain a wonderful quality of life, and lead *balanced* lives as well as fulfill our individual ministry calls. The personal, spiritual, and relational benefits have been extraordinary! Not only do we enjoy quality time with each other and Jake, but we are doing the very things we love most and are best skilled to do. Though there has been much discussion about the need for *quality* time in relationship building, we believe that both the *quantity* time and the *quality* time make our relationship exciting, satisfying, secure, and fun!

NEVER QUIT!

I'll never forget some scary words I heard from a young friend the week before her wedding. She said, "Well, if it doesn't work, we'll just get a divorce!"

Unfortunately, too many couples are going to the altar with the thought in the back of their minds that if the relationship doesn't work, they will get divorced. We live in an age and society where the tide is moving to prenuptial agreements, broken contracts, litigation, annulments, and irreconcilable differences. This tide is eroding our values as a country, destroying the family and the sanctity of marriage. People would rather quit than change or fight for their relationship.

It is normal to want to quit when we get discouraged or feel overwhelmed, or when a situation feels hopeless.

Every relationship will have experiences that yield discouraging, hopeless feelings. Admittedly some relationships will have more difficulties than others. Therefore, it is important to acknowledge that marriage is difficult *and* to make decisions that will help us succeed. We believe that making a nonnegotiable decision to never divorce is essential to keeping at bay the temptations that inevitably try to threaten all marriages.

Why is it important to make such a strong decision? Because we live in a society that is uncommitted. We cancel our agreements, return our goods, and get our money back. We have taken the fickleness in all aspects of society and adapted it to marriage. The rate of divorce has tripled since the 1960s, and more than 60 percent of new marriages are failing.[1]

Decide Not to Use the "D" Word

A strong decision never to divorce will give safety and security to a relationship. It provides the marriage an environment for intimacy and bonding. But you need to take your commitment a step farther. When Roger and I got married more than twenty years ago, we decided to never use the "D" word: *divorce*. We felt that even using the *word* would be damaging to our relationship. We didn't want to open the door, even a crack, to let the thought enter our minds. We have kept our word. Closing the door to the very mention of divorce prevented us from even considering bailing out when difficult adjustments and personal differences surfaced. It forced us to search for ways to change, cope, and grow. When we would otherwise choose to abandon, we choose to stay connected and work through our struggles.

Deciding never to quit or use the "D" word not only helps prevent the dissolving of marriages, but can actually be advantageous to a relationship. In *The Secret of Loving*, Josh McDowell cites research demonstrating that commitment to never quit on each other caused attraction to grow, the perceptions of the other person to change, and the individuals to become more loving toward each other.[2]

Roger and I backed up our general decision to never quit with some specific decisions that also helped ensure the success of our marriage. We decided to

- talk when we didn't want to,
- make love when we didn't necessarily feel like it,
- save when we wanted to spend,
- work when we would rather play,
- and go to church when we felt like sleeping in.

They were and are hard decisions! (We still have to make them!) They are seldom easy or fun, but they are *essential* to an effective marriage.

BECOME EACH OTHER'S BEST FRIEND AND BIGGEST ENCOURAGER

Laughing at your partner's dumbest jokes, playing games or sports together, enjoying each other's idiosyncrasies, bragging about your better half, and uplifting your spouse with your smile or hug are encouragements every person needs, yet often in the marriage relationship they get ignored. Fun, humor, affirmation, and encouragement are part of the friendship that a spouse should provide. Committing to a "best friend" relationship with your spouse sets the stage for intimacy. We have found that in addition to the financial, spiritual, and emotional support, marriage provides the perfect best friend for us.

Does That Mean We Can't Have Friends of the Opposite Sex?

Early in our marriage—and I can't exactly remember when—Roger and I discussed the fact that we needed to avoid having friends of the opposite sex with whom we would meet in private. In twenty years, we've had many friends, both singles and couples, with whom we socialize. But rarely have we met with these people in private. We enjoy friends and coworkers of the same and opposite sex, but to protect our relationship physically and emotionally, we decided not to confide in our friends or coworkers who are of the opposite sex regarding our marital relationship. We have taken this approach so that we avoid opening any intimate, emotional doors, setting wrong or inappropriate thoughts in motion, or compromising our relationship in any way.

A number of women have been Roger's secretary, and I have been on traveling speaking teams with men. But if or when either of us felt threatened or concerned, we shared our feelings and discussed additional boundaries that might be helpful to protect us. These types of decisions carry some feelings of resistance, but the benefits surpass the negative feelings.

The Three A's: Affirmation, Affection, and Apology

Because Roger does much premarital counseling as well as marriage counseling, he has come up with a system called the Three A's. As a counselor, Roger asks all of his couples to do the Three A's to help them stay connected on a daily basis. As a husband, he encourages us to do the same!

The Three A's are meant to encourage, lift, and love the other person. They are also a practical tool for catching up, patching up, and living up to one's promises. If the Three A's seem corny, *at times*, they are. (But humor often is good for a marriage!)

The Three A's are *affirmation, affection,* and *apology*. Here's how they work. Sometime during the day one person suggests that they do their Three A's. If it hasn't occurred by bedtime, then when the second person gets into bed, it becomes the final opportunity to do the Three A's.

The beauty of his system is that the entire process can be accomplished in three to five minutes. This relieves a couple from having to find a large quantity of time to achieve daily connection on days when time has not been available. Yet it is also a thread that can keep two lives connected!

The first *A* is *affirmation*.

One partner begins by sharing some behavior the other person did for which you are thankful, such as, "Thank you for helping me do the dishes tonight." Or you can share a quality that you like about the other person by saying, "Thank you for being so gentle with the girls."

As with all of our tools, there are a few rules about affirmations. (Broken rules during the Three *A*'s draw flags, similar to flags thrown during a football game when penalties transpire.) The first rule is not to use any negatives or discounts when giving affirmations. An example of an affirmation with a discount sounds like this: "I like the way you made dinner for me, but it sure would be nice if we could have that type of meal more often." The "but it sure would be nice if . . ." draws a flag. An affirmation cannot contain a negative discount factor. A flag would also be thrown for a statement such as, "Thank you for taking the time to sit at the table and listen to me when you came home from work, *but* I wish you hadn't left the table so soon to go into the den to read the newspaper." When you add the word *but*, you are certain to be breaking a rule! Keep the affirmation purely encouraging.

Here are some examples of positive affirmations:

- "Thank you for taking the time to sit at the table and talk with me after dinner. I appreciated it very much."
- "Thank you for working so hard and providing for our family. We are so fortunate to have such loving support from you."
- "I love the way you dress."
- "I felt so special when you hugged me in front of your friends. Thank you!"
- "I felt so loved when you brought me flowers. Thank you!"
- "Thank you for being so sensitive to my feelings."

- "I admire your generosity."
- "I respect your intelligence. I think you are a very wise person."

The second *A* is *affection*.

During this time, the goal is to have a time of intentional affection! It is time to give a hug, some form of physical touch, or even a gift. For married couples, it might move right into a sexual experience, or it might merely be the touch of toes, a hug, or a kiss. Here are some forms of the second *A*:

- Hugging
- Kissing
- Back rubs
- Loving caresses
- Flowers
- Notes
- Cards
- Gifts
- Verbal affection ("I love you" or "You mean the world to me")

The third *A* is *apology*.

The Bible tells us not to go to sleep holding on to our anger. During this time, you say that you are sorry for any hurt you may have caused the other person. Be very specific with the words you choose.

For instance, it would be appropriate to say, "I'm sorry for hurting you by . . . Will you forgive me?"

You are not trying to get too deep into hurts during this three- to five-minute exercise. There will undoubtedly be other times in a given day or week when you delve into hurts that require the use of the conflict resolution and forgiveness processes. You don't go as deep during the daily time designated for the Three *A*'s because you want to keep the exercise fairly short and positive. If you realize that you're going to need more time to resolve a difficult issue, then you could say something like, "We need to find a time to resolve this. What would be a good time to talk about this tomorrow?" Once again, bigger issues should ideally be resolved at times designated or, whenever possible, right at the moment. The third *A* is to respond to infractions that were overlooked or that occurred when there was not time to handle them or deal with them.

Begin the apology by stating how you think you hurt the other person. If nothing comes to mind, then ask the other person if you did anything that hurt him or her today. If the other person honestly didn't feel hurt that day, it is appropriate to respond, "I can't think of anything!"

Realistically, people in close relationships who spend significant amounts of time together will say or do things that hurt each other almost every day. In most cases, people don't hurt with intention. *They hurt because they are hurt, irritated, or frustrated.*

Here are a few examples of how to share the third *A*:

- "I'm sorry for being crabby when I came home from work. Will you forgive me?"
- "I'm sorry for being so short with you about your driving. Will you forgive me?"
- "I'm sorry for not noticing that you were all dressed up to go out. Will you forgive me?"

I'm going to be honest with you. Since Roger and I have been married so many years and we know each other's tendencies and personality traits, I *usually initiate* the Three A's. *And* if he did something to bug me that day, I will often cut right to the chase, name his infraction, and forgive him *before* he even has a chance to apologize! He rolls his eyes, and we usually laugh. This little pattern has a way of making his third *A* easier for both of us!

The commitment to do the Three A's daily must be mutual. In addition, keeping the time limit to three to five minutes will assure continual success with the system. If you need or want more time for discussion, do so at a later time, always keeping the Three A's as a separate time. We have found many couples, including ourselves, have increased their intimacy—and stayed connected on a daily basis—by sticking to this simple, short process. Some couples do the Three A's seven days a week. Others are committed to the process for three to five days a week. We'd encourage you to try a few different combinations, evaluate what works best for you, then stick to it!

If you can persuade another couple to do or begin the Three A's system, you can encourage and hold each other accountable to maintaining the process. You might call each other twice a week to remind the other couple to keep the system going. It's easy to stop even good things without encouragement and reminders.

ENCOURAGING YOU

The ideas we've shared with you represent the knowledge, skills, and decisions that we have studied, gleaned, practiced, and followed, resulting in twenty years of fidelity, fun, and faithfulness to God and each other! We want to assure you that our marriage has endured not because we are easygoing or exactly alike, but because we acknowledge our similarities and differences, and we work very hard at staying connected to God and each other.

Perhaps one of the greatest signs that our relationship is healthy and strong is that even after twenty years, I still consider Roger one of the wisest, kindest men I have ever met. I often joke that God did me a big favor (and saved me a lot of money) by allowing me to marry a counselor! His willingness to listen to, counsel, care for, and encourage me has never wavered or waned from the first day we met. Therefore, Roger's willingness to follow the biblical principle of loving me unconditionally, just as the Bible says Christ loves us, has caused me to respond to him with deep respect and love. What we've taught, we've lived and want to encourage you to try because it works! And it takes work!

Since Roger and I can't live without each other, we want to be *successful* at living with each other. We hope that the knowledge, skills, and decisions that we have shared with you will inspire you to join us in this adventure of living successfully with your spouse.

Chapter Eight

DO YOU KNOW HOW TO FIGHT A GOOD FIGHT?*

Dr. Les Parrott and Dr. Leslie Parrott

I have a brain, you know!" I yelled.

"I'm trying to help you, if you'd let me," Les replied.

Our voices seemed to echo through the entire city of San Francisco, where we were on a weekend trip with our friends, Randy and Pam. We were trying to catch a streetcar when one of our most explosive conflicts erupted.

It was our third attempt to jump onto a crowded trolley as it reached the crest of a hill. Les, with me holding on to his arm, leaped first to secure a position, but I, for the third time now, pulled back at the last moment.

"This is crazy!" I shouted.

"Just trust me; I know what I'm doing," Les coaxed.

The tension was palpable. Randy and Pam, watching the argument from its inception, stood still. Eventually, in their embarrassment, they crossed the street to escape our hollering.

"Why won't you just trust me?" Les demanded.

As the entire group of moving trolley passengers craned their heads to watch this marital match, I offered a retort that has since become infamous in our household: "I trust God for my safety, but I can't trust you!"

We seem to have our biggest arguments in public. On another occasion we were late for a weekend marriage retreat—and we

---

*Adapted from *Saving Your Marriage Before It Starts* by Dr. Les Parrott III and Dr. Leslie Parrott. Copyright © 1995 by Les and Leslie Parrott. Used by permission.

were the speakers. Leslie was still in her office pulling together some last-minute materials, and I (Les) was waiting impatiently in the car.

"Okay, Parrott, don't lose it," I murmured to myself. "She will be out any minute now; just relax and don't get angry at her." Five minutes turned into fifteen. "Here she comes now; just bite your tongue."

It was raining lightly as Leslie climbed into the car. But as she reached to close the car door, her armful of notes and hundreds of handouts slipped away, some into a curbside puddle, most scattering across the wet street.

I couldn't contain myself. "That's it," I said sternly. "I can't believe this! What are we going to do now? Couldn't you see that—"

"You're the one that wanted to do this retreat," Leslie interrupted.

"Oh, don't give me that. You—" My raised voice suddenly stopped as I tried to swallow my sentence. With the car door swung open wide and papers flying everywhere, I suddenly realized our derogatory remarks were being heard by several colleagues who were passing by. Keeping their eyes straight ahead, they pretended not to notice the "marriage experts" having their tiff, but there was no denying that the Parrotts were having a blowup. As we said, we have a knack for doing our "best" fighting in public.

Misunderstanding is a natural part of marriage. No matter how deeply a man and woman love each other, they will eventually have conflict. It is simply unrealistic to expect that both people will always want the same thing at the same time. Conflict in marriage is inevitable.

If you aren't married yet, this may not make a lot of sense. But it will. Thirty-seven percent of newlyweds admit to being more critical of their mates after being married. And thirty percent report an increase in arguments.[1] Stressed-out, dual-career couples today have more to negotiate than ever, and the potential for conflict is at every turn. But for couples who know how to work it out, conflict can actually lead to a deepening sense of intimacy. The trick is knowing how to argue.

Let's make this perfectly clear: *Knowing how to fight fair is critical to your survival as a happy couple.* Love itself is not enough to sustain a relationship in the jungle of modern life. Being in love is, in fact, a very poor indicator of which couples will stay married. Far more important to the survival of a marriage, research shows, is how well couples handle disagreements.[2] Many couples don't know how to handle conflict. Some mistake calmness and quiet for marital harmony and go out of their way to smooth over differences without really resolving them. Others, having watched their parents explode at each other, learn the wrong ways of fighting, and their arguments quickly degenerate into insults and abuse.

In this chapter we will show you how to fight fair and reduce your toxic quarrel quotient. We will begin our "combat training" by exploring the common issues that trip up couples. Then we will highlight the four lethal conflict styles you should stay clear of. Next we will tell you why fighting can be good for your marriage, and finally we will give you the "rules" for fighting a good fight.

WHAT COUPLES FIGHT ABOUT

So what are the thorny issues that cause couples to battle each other? Money? Sex? In-laws? Not always. It generally takes very little for the fur to fly in most marriages. It's the minor, almost embarrassing problems that tear at the fabric of a marriage.

Three days into their Florida vacation, Mike and Becky were ready to pack up and go home. Instead of unwinding and enjoying each other's company, they spent all their time fighting: He got sand all over the bottle of sunscreen; she wanted to sit on the beach, and he wanted to stay by the pool; she took too long getting ready to go out in the evening. When Mike and Becky arrived home a week later, both agreed that the vacation had been a complete disaster.

Why? Because they had argued about deep-felt issues? No. They simply bickered about things that didn't really matter.

The fact that most conflicts erupt over relatively minor issues, however, doesn't diminish the major ones. It seems there is a universal red alert that sounds in every marriage when certain topics are broached. Both happy and unhappy couples struggle with the same topics (although the struggles differ greatly in intensity and frequency).[3]

When it comes to the "big issue" list, research shows that money outranks all other topics as the number-one area of conflict among married couples.[4] Couples are constantly faced with financial decisions that cause them to ask, "Whose money is it?" What's surprising to many couples is that money fights are not a function of how much money they have or don't have. Couples fight about money no matter what their income is. Some couples argue over whether to go to Barbados or Europe for their vacation; other couples fight over whether they can afford a vacation at all.

Higher incomes can reduce stress, but they don't stop the fighting. Most couples, regardless of income, have conflicting spending and saving styles. One will be the big spender; the other will be the penny-pincher. Talking openly about money matters is probably the most difficult problem you and your partner will resolve. A good way to start is to discuss your spending styles with each other. How did your childhoods shape your beliefs about money? What are your spending priorities? Are they in sync with your partner's? Don't be disturbed if you find they conflict. The goal here is to compromise. If you let go of right-or-wrong thinking, it will be a lot easier to give and take.

WHAT UNHAPPY COUPLES DO WRONG

It's a Saturday morning in Seattle. Two newlyweds are finishing their Starbucks coffee while Bach's Brandenburg Concerto No.

4 plays on a state-of-the-art CD player. It is surprisingly sunny, and they find it hard to concentrate on reading the newspaper when they can watch pleasure boats glide by windows that overlook Lake Washington.

But something's different about this idyllic scene. Beneath the couple's casual clothes there are monitors taped to their skin, recording their heart rates. A different gadget measures their perspiration. Their every movement, facial expression, and conversation is being videotaped by three wall-mounted cameras and watched by observers hidden behind one-way glass. Tomorrow they'll have to give blood samples for additional analysis.

This is not a pleasant waterside apartment but a psychology lab at the University of Washington, and these newlyweds are subjects in a study conducted by Dr. John Gottman. Using high-tech equipment, Dr. Gottman and his team of researchers have been studying marriages for more than twenty years, identifying which ones will improve and which ones will deteriorate. They are now able to predict their results with an astounding ninety-five-percent accuracy rate.

Dr. Gottman can spot and track a couple's marital breakdown by observing how they handle conflict. When four bad omens appear in their conflict—what he calls "The Four Horsemen of the Apocalypse"—danger is imminent, for as each horseman arrives, he paves the way for the next. These four disastrous ways of interacting will sabotage your attempts to resolve conflict constructively. In order of least to most dangerous, they are: (1) criticism; (2) contempt; (3) defensiveness; and (4) stonewalling.[5]

Criticism

"I bought a VCR for about two hundred dollars at a warehouse sale. Molly took one look at it and blew up." Steve was telling us about a recent squabble, and Molly, his wife, was saying how she found herself complaining again and again about Steve's spending habits. Both of them agreed to be thrifty, but they had differing notions of what frugality meant. Steve didn't always turn off the lights when he left a room, for example, while Molly spent hours clipping coupons for their next trip to the grocery store. When Steve didn't measure up to her standards, Molly complained.

Were Molly's complaints justified? We think so. Not because she is right, but because she has the right to complain. Complaining is a healthy marital activity. Airing a complaint, though rarely pleasant, makes the marriage stronger in the long run than suppressing the complaint.

But Molly, without realizing it, had crossed a dangerous line. As time passed, she found that her comments did not lead Steve to change his spending habits. That's when something potentially damaging to their marriage occurred: Rather than complaining about his actions, she began to criticize him. "You never carry your weight. You do what you want, when. It's like living with a grown-up child."

There may not seem to be much difference between complaining and criticizing, but there is. Criticism involves attacking someone's personality rather than his behavior. As a general rule, criticism entails blaming, making a personal attack or an accusation, while a complaint is a negative comment about something you wish were otherwise. Complaints usually begin with the word *I* and criticisms with the word *you*. For example, "I wish we went out more than we do" is a complaint. "You never take me anywhere" is a criticism. Criticism is just a short hop beyond complaining, and it may seem like splitting hairs, but receiving a criticism really does feel far worse than receiving a complaint.

Contempt

By their first anniversary, Steve and Molly still hadn't resolved their financial differences. In the heat of one particularly nasty argument, Molly found herself shrieking, "Why are you always so irresponsible? You are so selfish!"

Fed up, Steve retorted, "Give me a break. You are so tight you squeak when you walk. I don't know how I ended up with you anyway." The second bad omen, contempt, had entered the scene.

Contempt will poison a relationship whether a couple has been together four months or forty years. What separates contempt from criticism, according to Gottman, "is the *intention to insult* and *psychologically abuse* your partner." There ought to be a law against contempt, because it is aimed right into the heart of a person and ends up destabilizing the relationship and causing pain. When contempt appears, it overwhelms the marriage and blots out every positive feeling partners have for each other. Some of the most common expressions of contempt are name-calling, hostile humor, and mockery. And once they have entered a home, the marriage goes from bad to worse.

Defensiveness

Once Steve and Molly acted contemptuously, defensiveness entered the picture and made matters worse. They both felt victimized by the other, and neither was willing to take responsibility for setting things right. Who can blame them? If you are being bombarded with insults, the natural inclination is to defend yourself: "It's not my fault. You were supposed to pay that bill, not me." One of the reasons defensiveness is so destructive is that it becomes a reflex. The "victim"—reacting instinctively—doesn't see anything wrong with being defensive, but defensiveness tends to escalate a conflict rather than resolve it. Every time either Steve or Molly felt completely righteous in their stance, every time they made excuses and denied responsibility, they added to their marital misery.

Stonewalling

Steve and Molly were nearing rock bottom. Exhausted and overwhelmed by Molly's attacks, Steve eventually stopped responding, even defensively, to her accusations. "You never say anything," Molly would scream. "You just sit there. It's like talking to a brick wall." Steve usually didn't react at all. On some occasions he would shrug his shoulders as if to say, "I can't get anywhere with you, so why try?"

Most stonewallers (about 85 percent of them) are men. Feeling overwhelmed by emotions, they start withdrawing by presenting a "stone wall" response. They try to keep their faces immobile, avoid eye contact, hold their necks rigid, and avoid nodding their heads or making the small sounds that would indicate they are listening. Stonewallers often claim they are trying not to make things worse, but they do not seem to realize that stonewalling itself is a very powerful act. It conveys disapproval, icy distance, and smugness.

Stonewalling need not mark the end of a marriage, but once routine interactions have deteriorated to this extent, the marriage will be very fragile and will require a good deal of hard work to save.

Keep in mind that anyone may stonewall or become defensive, contemptuous, or critical. Even with very happy couples these behaviors happen occasionally during an intense marital conflict. The real danger here is letting these ways of interacting become a habit.

WHY A GOOD FIGHT AIN'T SO BAD

Conflict is a social taboo, considered morally wrong by some. The assumption that conflict doesn't belong in healthy relationships is based partly on the idea that love is the polar opposite of hate. But emotional intimacy involves feelings of both love and hate, of wanting to be close and needing to be separate, of agreeing and disagreeing.

The absence of fights does not augur well for most marriages. Partners who refuse to accept conflict as a part of marriage miss opportunities to creatively challenge and be challenged by each other. They also risk more negative consequences. Unresolved, unhandled conflict acts as a cancer that erodes the passion, intimacy, and commitment of marriage. Couples who do not "make an issue of things" often resort to "anger substitutes" rather than dealing directly with their emotions. They will overeat, get depressed, gossip, or suffer physical illness. While these substitutes may be more socially acceptable than the direct expression of anger, they can result in what experts call a "devitalized marriage," where false intimacy is the most couples can hope for.[6] A typical evening in the home of a nonfighting couple who has been suppressing anger for years might look like this:

He:	*(yawning)* How was your day, dear?
She:	*(pleasantly)* Okay, how was yours?
He:	Oh, you know, the usual . . .
She:	Anything special you want to do later?
He:	Oh, I don't know . . .

Nothing more meaningful is exchanged for the rest of the evening because the energy these two use to repress their anger drains their relationship of vitality. They evade conflict altogether by "gunnysacking," keeping their grievances secret while tossing them into an imaginary gunnysack that grows heavier and heavier over time. And when marital complaints are toted and nursed along quietly in a gunnysack for any length of time, they make a dreadful mess when they burst.

The point is that marital conflict is a necessary challenge to be met rather than avoided. We'll say it again: *Conflict is natural in intimate relationships.* Once this is understood, conflict no longer represents a crisis but an opportunity for growth.

David and Vera Mace, prominent marriage counselors, observed that on the day of marriage, people have three kinds of raw material to work with. First there are the things you have in common, the things you both like. Second are the things in which you are different, but the differences are complementary. And third, there are the differences that are not at all complementary and cause most of your conflict. Every married couple has differences that are not complementary—lots of them. As you and your partner move closer together, those differences become more prominent. You see, conflict can be the result of growing closer together. As we have said to many couples in counseling: Conflict is the price you pay for deepening intimacy. But when you learn to fight fair, your marriage can flourish.

FIGHTING THE GOOD FIGHT

Suppose there were a formula for a happy marriage—would you follow it? Of course, who wouldn't? Especially if the formula were backed up by hard evidence that proved its success.

Well, the astonishing news is that such a formula now exists, thanks to pioneering research done with thousands of couples around the country. Psychologists Howard Markman and Scott Stanley at the University of Denver have predicted, with eighty-percent accuracy, who will be divorced six or seven years after marrying. And what they look for is not *whether* a couple argues, but *how* the couple argues.[7]

We now know not only what unhappy couples are doing wrong when they argue, but what happy couples are doing right. Successful couples resolve conflict without leaving scars, because they have learned to fight a good fight by sticking closely to the following rules.

Don't Run from Strife

We need to consider the story of the genie in the bottle who, during his first thousand years of incarceration, thinks, *Whoever lets me out will get three wishes,* and who, during his second thousand years of incarceration, thinks, *Whoever lets me out I'm gonna kill.* Many of us, like that genie, seem to get meaner and more dangerous the longer our grievances are bottled up. Don't allow yourself to bury something that irritates you. Repressed irritations have a high rate of resurrection.

Happy couples may disagree vehemently, but they don't shut their partners out. When one spouse brings up an issue, the other listens attentively. From time to time, the listener will paraphrase what the other says ("You're worried about our overspending?") to make sure the message is understood.

Choose Your Battles Carefully

Love may be blind, but for many partners marriage is a magnifying glass. Couples who are virtually certain to break up can't seem to find a relaxed, reasonably efficient way of figuring out how to settle differences as small as which movie to see or whose friends to visit. Eventually, their inability to negotiate does them in, no matter how much in love they are. So take the experts' advice and choose your battles carefully.

You've probably seen the "grant me the wisdom to accept the things I cannot change" prayer on plaques and posters. It's over-familiar, but it's true: One of the major tasks of marriage is learning what can and should be changed (habits of nagging, for example) and what should be overlooked (the way a spouse squeezes the toothpaste tube).

We often tell couples that about ninety percent of the issues that they bicker about can probably be overlooked. We know how easy it is to criticize one's mate. We ourselves have done our fair share of yapping about minor infractions, but we've also learned not to sweat the small stuff. This simple advice can keep you from ruining a Friday evening or even an entire vacation. So before you gripe about the way your partner made the bed or cleared the table, ask yourself if it's worth it.

Define the Issue Clearly

Shari and Ron seemed addicted to friction. Their most recent blowup occurred while entertaining a group of friends in their home. Everyone was having a good time, enjoying the conversation and the food. As Shari started to serve the dessert, Ron offered to pour the coffee. Shari appreciated his offer and went into the kitchen to get a few more plates. When she returned to the dining room, Ron was still talking and hadn't started serving the coffee. Disgusted, Shari made a derogatory comment, and the two of them began arguing.

"There they go again," said one of the guests.

Embarrassed, Shari and Ron suddenly stopped fighting. After the guests were gone, Shari asked Ron, "Do we fight that frequently?"

Ron nodded soberly. Both he and Shari knew they fought too much, but they didn't know why.

Many couples find themselves bickering on a regular basis over just about anything—no issue is too small, or too big, to spar over. When Shari and Ron came to see us, we gave them a simple assignment that reduced the frequency of their arguing almost immediately. It was this: When you feel the tension rising, ask each other to define clearly what the fight is about until both of you understand the issue. Marital battles become habitual if the source of the conflict is not identified, but once couples define the issue, they can be more up front about what is really bugging them. And once the conflict is clearly defined, it often takes care of itself.

At Ron and Shari's dinner fiasco, for example, Shari was not really arguing about having to do all the work herself. She felt angry at Ron for playing basketball earlier in the day when he promised to be home with her, and arguing in front of their friends was a way of getting back at him. Once Ron understood the real issue, he could empathize with Shari's frustration and was better able to repair it.

To identify the real source of a conflict, you must address the questions "What are we really quarreling about?" and "What is the real source of our disagreement?" When couples do not address or cannot answer these questions, the quarrel is often displaced to another topic ("And another thing: Why do you always . . . ?"). So before you fight, be sure you know what you are fighting about.

State Your Feelings Directly

Sonia, married just over a year, was continually fighting with her husband about his hectic travel schedule. "I don't understand why your job takes priority over our relationship," she told him over the phone one evening. As he began to explain the pressure of an impending deadline and why he was having to travel so much, it suddenly struck Sonia that she did not really resent him for being gone and working so hard; all she really wanted was for him to say, "I miss you. I feel terrible about not being home. And you're such a fabulous person for being able to handle everything while I'm away." Once she stated her feelings directly, she got what she wanted.

We often teach couples the "X, Y, Z" formula to help them state their feelings. Think of this approach as a kind of game in which you fill in the blanks with your particular gripe in mind: "In situation X, when you do Y, I feel Z." For example, "When you are on the road (X), and you don't tell me that you miss me (Y), I feel unloved and lonely (Z)." Or, "Last Thursday night (X) when you called your mom long distance and talked for a half hour (Y), I felt upset because we can't afford those long calls (Z)." Using this formula will help you avoid insults and character assassination, allowing you instead to simply state how your partner's behavior affects your feelings.

Another example would be, "When we are riding in the car (X) and you change the radio station without asking me first (Y),

I feel hurt that my desires are not considered (Z)." That is far more constructive to your partner than saying "You never consider my feelings when it comes to music." Although the latter may be what first comes to your mind, it's likely to draw a defensive response that gets you nowhere.

Rate the Intensity of Your Feelings

We have observed that one partner in the couples we counsel is often more expressive than the other. In other words, one person articulates his or her feelings more quickly and more intensely than the other. And we have seen this imbalance cause problems time and again because what is very important to one person may appear not to be very important at all.

When James and Karen were setting up their first apartment, Karen wanted to paint the kitchen walls a light blue. She brought home paint samples to show her new husband, but he didn't share her excitement:

"I found the perfect color," Karen said enthusiastically, holding paint chips up to the wall.

"I'm not really crazy about it," Jim said.

"Oh, you'll like it once you see it on the wall. It'll be great."

"I don't know."

The phone rang in the middle of their discussion, and that was the last they talked about it. Three days later, James couldn't believe his eyes when he came home to a light blue kitchen. "What's this?" he exclaimed. "I thought we agreed not to paint it this color!"

"You said you didn't care, so I went ahead."

"I never said that!"

For the rest of the evening, James and Karen argued over feeling betrayed and unappreciated. But the whole scuffle could have been prevented if they knew just how important (or unimportant) the issue of painting the kitchen was to each of them. As it turned out, James didn't express it well, but he felt very strongly about not painting the kitchen light blue. Karen, on the other hand, was excited and eager to set up house. She could have very easily been talked into another color. Their feelings and how they expressed them were almost polar opposites.

There is a simple technique that could have prevented much of James and Karen's grief. For several years now, we have been handing out hundreds of what we call "Conflict Cards." Using this small plastic card, no bigger than a credit card, helps put couples on even ground when it comes to expressing the intensity of their feelings. We are not sure where the idea for this card came from, but it has helped us resolve plenty of conflicts in our own marriage, and we have seen it work for hundreds of others.

What's on the card? It's simple, really. On the card is a scale from one to ten ranking the intensity of a person's feelings:

1. I'm not enthusiastic, but it's no big deal to me.
2. I don't see it the way you do, but I may be wrong.
3. I don't agree, but I can live with it.
4. I don't agree, but I'll let you have your way.
5. I don't agree and cannot remain silent on this.
6. I do not approve, and I need more time.
7. I strongly disapprove and cannot go along with it.
8. I will be so seriously upset I can't predict my reaction.
9. No possible way! If you do, I quit!
10. Over my dead body!

Anytime a heated exchange occurs, a couple can simply pull out this list and rank the depth of their disagreement. ("This is a three for me." "It's a five for me.") By rating their conflict, they can play on a level field even when one person is more expressive than the other.

If you would like a free Conflict Card, please call Zondervan DirectSource at 1–800–727–3480.

By the way, we tell couples who use the Conflict Card that if both partners rank an issue at seven or higher, they should seek objective help from a marriage therapist.

Give Up Put-downs

Remember the childhood saying: "Sticks and stones can break my bones, but names will never hurt me"? That's a lie—names do hurt, as many unhappy couples can testify. Unfortunately, couples are generally experts at character assassination ("You don't want a better job because you're lazy").

Put-downs are especially lethal when they attack an Achilles' heel. If your spouse has confessed to you that his cruel high-school classmates nicknamed him "egghead," and if, in adulthood, he still has fears about being socially clumsy, that name is off-limits. Two Achilles' heels that are mentioned so often that they must be universal are sexual performance and parents. It is tricky enough, in life's mellowest moments, to discuss sexual dissatisfaction with a mate, but to use it in an argument is a rotten idea. And even though we are allowed to criticize our own parents, it's dirty pool for a spouse to be doing it.

One of the sad facts of close relationships is that we treat the ones we love worse than we treat just about anyone else. We are more likely to hurl insults at our marriage partner than any other person in our life. We are even more polite to acquaintances than we are to our mates. Here are a few tips for cultivating politeness in your marriage:

- When your partner has done a chore, always show appreciation for the job even if the way it was done doesn't meet with your approval (say, "Thanks for washing the car" rather than "You missed a spot").
- Surround mealtimes with pleasant conversations. Shut off the TV and pay attention to your mate instead.

Research has shown that it takes only one put-down to undo hours of kindness that you give to your partner. So the most gracious offering of politeness you can give your partner is to avoid put-downs altogether.

Don't Dwell on Downers

If you are having a fight about how much time your partner is spending at work, we promise you that it will not advance your argument if you also note that he or she is overdrawn at the bank and always leaves you the car with no gas in the tank. Stick closely to the relevant issues—and *try to end the fight*. Refocus the exchange when it gets off course ("Look, let's just decide who's dropping this off at the dry cleaners. Later we can talk about how the laundry gets done at home."). Try to calm your partner down ("Let's take a break. We're both too upset to discuss this reasonably right now."). Unhappy couples turn every spat into a slippery slope of one unkind word that leads to another:

He: I guess my mistake was looking forward to a nice dinner.

She: If you came home on time, you might have gotten one. You care more about your job than about me.

He: Somebody's gotta make a living.

She: It wouldn't be you if I didn't work like a dog to put you through school!

This kind of runaway spleen-venting is one of the strongest predictors of divorce. These couples veer off into heated, unproductive fighting over tangential or old, unresolved issues. They resolve nothing, and negative feelings rage.

In stable marriages, the other partner won't always retaliate when unfairly provoked. Instead, they find ways to defuse tension:

He: I was really looking forward to a decent meal!
She: Your hours are so unpredictable I can't plan one.
He: There's no choice. I'm under a lot of pressure at work.
She: Well, for tonight, should we just order pizza?

It's not how you get into arguments but how you exit them. If you dwell on downers you will eventually sink.

Let's face it: All is not fair in love and war. Clean and constructive fighting is better than down and dirty fighting, that's for sure. Though of course we are bound to slip, trying to follow the above "rules" will help you fight a good fight.

Chapter Nine

THE UNION FIDELITY LOVE BANK IS ALWAYS OPEN*

Dr. Kevin Leman

The extramarital affair is the most tragic result of unmet needs in a marriage. Whenever I deal with a couple who have been torn apart by his infidelity or hers, I can always count on one thing: Details of the affair will tell me exactly what is wrong within that marriage. I call it the Marital Litmus Test because it clearly reveals what is lacking in the relationship.

A straying wife will tell me, "John was so attentive before we got married, but in a few months everything changed. At least Bruce would talk to me. I was starved for that. The afternoon we wound up in bed was after we had a long talk about what it takes to be fulfilled."

Or a husband with a mistress will say: "My wife hasn't been interested in sex in years. I didn't mean to fall in love with Shirley, but working together day after day . . ."

Affairs are often depicted in films or television shows as therapeutic "one-night stands" or brief flings to let off steam.

"Yes, I had an affair," the heroine tells her friend at lunch, "but now it's over, and I'm able to cope at home a little better."

I suppose this kind of thing happens in real life as well as in soap operas, but the affairs that come to my attention arise out of deep unmet needs at home. There are two key words that describe every hard-core affair: *disillusionment* and *license*.

---

*Adapted from Kevin Leman, *Keeping Your Family Together When the World Is Falling Apart* (New York: Delacorte, 1992). Used by permission.

Typically, disillusionment sets in because he is starved for sex or she is starved for affection and conversation. I say "typically" because sometimes it is precisely the reverse: the wife complains about not having any sex, or he complains about a lack of communication.

Whatever the complaints of either partner, their disillusionment is plain. Before marriage they think they will have the perfect life: openness, sharing, doing everything together—and of course terrific lovemaking. And it seems to work out that way for a few months, maybe even a few years. But then the children arrive, schedules change, and life gets busier. Soon they are going their own separate ways, passing each other like two radarless ships in the night, and intimacy becomes a vague memory.

In most cases, one spouse tires of the disillusionment first and decides she or he deserves better. "I have a right to meet my needs," says the disappointed spouse, and consciously or unconsciously, this husband or wife starts navigating toward ports of call where other arms are open. Disillusionment leads to license, a feeling you can get when life doesn't work out and you begin to think, *I have the right to do things my way.* And when a spouse gets that disillusioned, it often leads to deep involvement with someone else.

INTIMACY DIES OF SHEER NEGLECT

For any affair to start, there must first be the erosion and rusting of something very important at home—what I call the "intimate connection."

In many marriages, when the intimacy connection goes, an affair takes its place. It seems there is always someone waiting in the wings—or at the watercooler at the office—who is more than willing to fill the void. And this someone seems to meet the needs that are not being met in a marriage that started full of promise and is now as empty as a house the day after the movers have come and gone. Or perhaps a better analogy is that the Love Bank is now empty, with both partners' accounts at zero.

THE LOVE BANK IS ALWAYS OPEN

In *His Needs, Her Needs,* Willard Harley uses a Love Bank analogy to describe what happens as a man and woman meet for the first time, start to date, fall in love, get married, and then move in one of two directions: toward more and more intimacy, or toward the destruction of intimacy and very possibly the tragedy of divorce, triggered by one partner's affair (and sometimes both).[1]

Harley believes that every person has an emotional recorder deep inside, which he calls the Love Bank. This recorder registers the effects of positive and negative experiences, which cause deposits and withdrawals of "love units." Every person you know has an account in your Love Bank, and your spouse should be the major account holder of all.

When a husband does something to make his wife comfortable, he gets a deposit worth one unit in her Love Bank. If he makes her feel good, he gets a two; making her feel very good gets him a three; and super terrific rates him a plus four. But if he makes her uncomfortable, it's a minus one; if he makes her feel bad, it's a minus two; very bad, minus three; and terrible and depressed would result in a withdrawal of four units from her Love Bank.

Meanwhile, his wife is doing banking of her own. What she does to make him feel comfortable or uncomfortable, good or not so good, very good or very bad, and terrific or horrible all register as deposits in, and withdrawals from, his Love Bank, where she has her account.

Harley admits that the Love Bank is an artificial device, but it describes perfectly what goes on during every waking moment of a marriage.

The Love Bank concept gets particularly interesting when you realize that different husbands and wives register deposits and withdrawals differently. What may be an "uncomfortable" encounter for one partner may be a "feel very bad" encounter for the other. What may be a "feel good" encounter for one can be a "terrific" experience for the other. That's why it's so important to know your partner, be aware of the different ways you react to each other and the rest of the world, and then say and do the positive things that keep both Love Banks in the marriage filled to overflowing. There is no better way to affair-proof your marriage than that.

In the rest of this chapter I focus on using three simple strategies to affair-proof your marriage:

1. avoiding temptation,
2. rekindling romance, and
3. developing couple power.

All three of these strategies are based on Reality Discipline.[2] That's why they're simple, but that doesn't necessarily mean they're easy. Using Reality Discipline is often difficult but always worthwhile. And the more you use it, the easier it gets.

WANDER NOT INTO TEMPTATION

When Steve Kerr tried out for the University of Arizona basketball team, it was obvious he was a great shot, particularly from twenty feet and beyond. But he also had some liabilities. As Coach Lute Olson put it tongue-in-cheek, "He's short, but he's slow."

Kerr got his chance, however, and went on to become one of the best three-point shooters in college history. After helping lead the Wildcats to the final four NCAA tournament in 1988, Kerr signed with the Phoenix Suns of the NBA. Later, he was traded to the Cleveland Cavaliers, who wanted to use him as a three-point specialist. In 1990 he posted one of the best three-point shooting marks in the league.

How could someone who isn't all that tall and not gifted with natural speed be so effective in the toughest competition on earth? Lute Olson summed it up best when he said, "The key to using Steve is to keep him out of situations where he is overmatched."

Olson's remark contains a nugget of wisdom for all of us, whether we play basketball, backgammon, or the game of life. If you want to affair-proof your marriage, *stay out of situations where you are overmatched.*

In other words, there are definitely times to say no—to working late in certain situations, to casual invitations to coffee, lunch, or dinner with certain people, to accepting certain little gifts or favors. To put it all another way, in Reality Discipline terms: "Know your limits. If you're a tricycle person, stay out of the fast lane."

ADMIT YOU CAN'T ALWAYS "HANDLE IT"

One of the best ways to stay aware of temptation and avoid the danger of being overmatched is to be sure you keep a strong spiritual influence working on your marriage. As I deal with people who have become entrapped in extramarital affairs, I often hear them admit, "I thought I could handle it," or, "I didn't think it would go that far," or, "I was trying to be a good friend. I didn't really know how lonely I was myself."

One of the greatest strengths and advantages to developing the spiritual values that you both practice together in church or synagogue weekly is that you learn that you can't always "handle it." You learn to know yourself and your weaknesses. Most important, you learn you can call on spiritual resources for strength.

Because some people immediately link the word *spiritual* with religion, they complain that they may wind up on a guilt trip. My answer, which may sound a bit odd coming from a psychologist, is, "What's wrong with a little healthy guilt?"

If your spiritual values are really important to you, it's entirely possible that God's still, small voice might speak to you when you don't realize you are about to drift into a situation where you are definitely out of your depth. If you feel a bit of guilt at that point, I say that's all to the good. Better to feel a twinge of guilt and stay out of trouble than wander into an affair that will cause a flood of guilt later.

FATIGUE CAN MAKE A FOOL OF ANYONE

But as you develop your spiritual resources, don't be a spendthrift with your physical and emotional resources. In other words, don't get so busy, so weary and run-down, that you aren't thinking very straight.

Keep in mind what Vince Lombardi, legendary coach of the Green Bay Packers, once said: "Fatigue makes cowards of us all." Fatigue can also make a fool out of anyone. When you tear through life overscheduled, overcommitted, and overworked, your resistance has to drop. And when resistance is low, you can catch just about anything. Ironically, when a person's resistance is low, it is often then that that person takes temptation too lightly and wanders into questionable or even dangerous territory.

Even ministers can fall into the fatigue trap. In fact, they are often more vulnerable because they are notorious for working long hours, trying to handle too many things, trying to please too many people. As I was talking to a pastor in a church where I was conducting a weekend seminar, he took me aside to say confidentially, "Kevin, these people are killing me."

"What people? Are you talking about people in your church?"

"Yes—that's exactly who I'm talking about. I—"

Just then a woman hurried up and interrupted our conversation: "Pastor, can I see you right now?"

The pastor looked at me as if to say, "See what I mean?"

Making a spur-of-the-moment decision, I turned to the lady and said, "I'm sorry, the pastor can't talk to you right now. I'm sure if you call the church on Monday, he'll be able to set a time for you."

The woman blinked and looked at me as if to say, "And *who* are you?"

Actually, she knew very well who I was—the speaker for the weekend. Proceeding to stare right through me, she turned back to her pastor to repeat her request: "But Pastor, it won't take but a minute. I just want to see you about—"

"No, seriously," I interrupted her again. "He really can't talk to you right now."

With that the lady let out a loud "Hmmmph!" and stalked away in what I assumed was a huff.

"I can't believe you said that!" my pastor friend said incredulously.

"I probably lost a participant in my seminar, but I did it for one reason," I explained. "That's exactly what you're going to have to do—get better at saying no to people, or all your good intentions and work will go against you, and you won't have anything left for your own family."

As far as I know, this pastor wasn't in danger of wandering into an affair, but who knows what pressures were really working on him? When you are tired, hassled, and feeling like your own church flock is "killing you," anything can happen and often does. I've had more than one pastor come to me for counseling after becoming enmeshed in an affair to say, "I don't know what happened. She had just gone through a divorce, and I was just trying to help her...."

SATISFIED PARTNERS DON'T WANDER

As you work on staying out of questionable situations yourself, do everything you can to help your partner do the same thing.

Although there is no one-hundred-percent guarantee, as a general rule, satisfied partners do not wander.

One of the best "satisfied partner" illustrations I ever saw was on a *Donahue* show that focused on fidelity versus infidelity in marriage. Well into the program, a cute little old lady who must have been close to eighty got up to tell the audience that her husband had died recently, but she looked back at fifty-five years of marital happiness. How had they done it? I can't recall her exact words, but she said something to the effect of, "I got all the juices out of him and didn't leave any for anyone else."

There was a roar of laughter, but people weren't laughing at her—they were laughing with her, because they knew her words were full of wisdom. If marriage partners are getting enough attention, affection, and sexual fulfillment at home, they are not likely to stray into an affair.

WHAT IF YOU ARE THINKING OF CHUCKING IT ALL?

As I share these different ideas of how to stay away from temptation, I am well aware that some readers are so discouraged, they are not even sure they *want* to stay away from temptation. They don't feel there is much of their marriage to save, and they've lost their will to work at it. I feel deep sympathy for this problem, but as I counsel people who have reached the point where they are ready to chuck it all and have a fling, I don't use sympathy—I switch to some hard-nosed Reality Discipline.

"I know how empty you must feel," I respond. "I know you believe you have a right to happiness and fulfillment. But think of the children—your four-year-old or your five-year-old. Imagine yourself holding them on your knee and explaining that you're not all going to be living together anymore. That Mommy and

Daddy haven't been getting along too well and that you have found somebody else."

Some clients think this kind of speech is "hitting below the belt." Maybe it is, but then, so is having an affair. Think it through carefully before you take the plunge, and remember that the whole is always more important than the parts—even your own parts.

In recent years it has been encouraging to see that divorce has been "going out of style" to some degree. Increasing numbers of people are realizing the high cost of "disposable marriages," particularly where children are involved. According to Bickley Townsend, a vice president in the organization that conducts the Roper poll, "there is definitely a turning-away from the acceptability of divorce and from minimizing the impact of divorce."

In 1990 the Roper poll asked two thousand people to define the most important aspect of success, and the top choice was "being a good wife and mother or husband and father." In 1986 the most popular answer to the same question had been, "Being true to yourself."[3]

Michele Weiner-Davis is one therapist who used to be overwhelmed by problems that husbands and wives shared in marital counseling, and she would suggest to them how they could "dissolve things peacefully." In recent years, however, she has switched to believing that it is better for people to do all they can to save their marriage.

Wiener-Davis, who now calls herself a "divorce buster," tries to help counselees be aware of the serious postdivorce problems they will face, such as disastrous financial situations for the woman and the pain and hurt for the children who may be involved. Years later, children may still have wounds that haven't healed. She also points out: "Half of first marriages and 60 percent of second marriages end in divorce. If people got rid of their problems by getting rid of their spouses, we wouldn't be seeing those statistics. Many people say, 'If I knew then what I know now, I'm not sure I would have gotten my divorce.'"[4]

ROMANCE KEEPS YOU OUT OF THE RUT

I'm glad the idea of working at marriages is back in vogue because, for me, "working at it" has been the cornerstone of Reality Discipline. While some situations are truly incredible, I begin every case assuming that there is hope if I can get both partners to agree to at least try to work at their relationship. The typical couple that comes for counseling is convinced that romance has long since faded from their marriage and cannot be revived. But I believe that any couple can do many things to make plenty of deposits in each other's Love Bank.

For example, I sometimes suggest to my clients, "Have you ever thought of keeping your mate off balance?" I realize this sounds a little odd. Why would marriage partners want to keep each other "off balance"? It all depends on how they do it and why.

If there is anything that kills romance, it is sameness. Every married couple experiences the "letdown" that follows the first glow and breathlessness of falling in love, tying the knot, and then discovering that reality seems to leave out romance. But it doesn't have to be that way if you are both committed to keeping each other off balance with little surprises that say in different ways, "I love you," "I'm proud of you," "I really like being married to you!" And sometimes the surprises can be big ones—wild and crazy stuff, perhaps, or just taking time to make a date or a weekend a lot more special and intimate.

THE NAKED LADY WHO NEEDED A LIFT

One of the more outstanding examples of the wild and crazy category that I've seen involved a couple whose marriage had gotten into the sexual doldrums. During a counseling session that I had alone with the wife, I mentioned to her that sometimes it really helps when the woman is more aggressive and takes a more active role in initiating sex. I never cease to marvel at what people can do with a rather simple suggestion.

Not many days later, this couple went to a party. Due to their busy schedules, they had to drive there separately. As the party ended, the wife managed to leave before the husband. She arrived home several minutes ahead of him at the long common driveway they shared with the family who lived next door. After going down this driveway almost a quarter of a mile, she pulled off to the side and removed every stitch of clothing she had on.

In a few minutes, she saw headlights turn into the driveway off the main highway, and she got out of the car and stood there, stark naked, with her thumb out as if she were hitchhiking. As the headlights approached, it occurred to her she hadn't reached the Y where the driveway split, with one part leading to her house and the other to the neighbor's. *What if this isn't my husband?* she thought. *What if it's the neighbor instead?*

But by then it was too late. The headlights caught her in their glare, the car stopped, and the door opened. Fortunately, it was her husband, who went along with the gag and asked, "Hey, lady, do you need a lift?"

Needless to say, this woman's willingness to do something wild and crazy gave their love life a lift—and then some! I've seen it happen so many times. When a woman becomes assertive and aggressive with her husband sexually, it does wonders for his self-esteem, and it puts her more in the mood for lovemaking as well.

On the other side of the coin, when a man tones down his natural male aggressiveness and gently centers his thoughts on pleasing his wife, she becomes more interested in sex and possibly becomes more aggressive herself. My first law for a strong family advises, "Always put your marriage first." A good corollary to that law says

> For more romance in most marriages, the wife should become more sexually aggressive, and the man should become more patient and gentle.

Hitchhiking naked and hoping your husband comes along first may not be your style, but there are other ways to do something a little crazy, if you are so inclined. One man, a friend of mine, came home from work and found his wife on the dresser, ready to leap into his arms. This might not sound very unusual in itself, but you must realize that she had dressed for the occasion in nothing but Saran Wrap! When my friend told me what had happened, my only explanation was that his wife might have been reading "one of those books" again (maybe it was one of mine!).

No matter—he admitted that he had had a lot of fun seeing how long it would take him to peel off the Saran Wrap. "Kevin, if you think getting Saran Wrap off a sweaty body is easy, just try it sometime!"

THE MORE CONVENTIONAL
APPROACH WORKS TOO

I doubted that Sande would be interested in Saran Wrap—that would be a little too rich for her own conservative firstborn tastes. She does, however, have more conventional ways of being very creative.

Recently, she and I wound up in Toronto, Canada, to celebrate our anniversary, and as we were about to head out for dinner, she said, "Let's just eat in the room. I've already ordered room service."

Because I was tired, I thought that sounded like a good idea, but things got even better. Sande excused herself and disappeared into the bathroom. About then, the dinner arrived, and after the bellhop left, Sande came out of the bathroom dressed in a very sexy, new red negligee. Then she reached into her purse and brought out a big beautiful red candle. In minutes its delightful fragrance filled the room as it illuminated our dinner together.

It was a wonderful evening—one I'll never forget. The four children were safe at home with relatives, and I was trapped in a hotel room with a beautiful woman in a red negligee. What made it especially memorable was Sande's extra planning and creativity, not to mention her aggressiveness, which tickles me as much as it does the next husband.

The moral of all these little stories is that husbands and wives should become very adept at surprising one another. All it takes is a little planning and then taking the trouble to pull it off. With these two simple principles in mind, anyone can cook up something that will be a surprise, something you can both talk about, laugh about, and enjoy long after it's over, because the memories of the good times you had together will be there. In other words, the Union Fidelity Love Bank will be operating on a deposit basis for both of you. Keep in mind that when you both have a super terrific time, deposits are made in *both* Love Banks, not just one. This is what the intimacy connection is all about.

Also remember that, while you may want to do a special production now and then, it's the little things that really matter. Little things like coming home early and taking her out to dinner at a place she really likes (not the Colonel). Like sending her a note home from the office—handwritten—that says, "I want you to know how much I care. I want you to know how much I appreciate all you do for our family. You do so much for me and for the children. I'm so proud of you."

And, of course, the notes can also flow in the other direction—from wife to husband. Don't forget that one of a husband's basic needs is admiration and respect. You'll never know how many points you can put in his Love Bank by slipping a note into his lunch or jacket pocket that says, "You're such a wonderful husband and such a great dad. The kids and I are so lucky that you belong to us."

There are endless ways to keep the spark of romance burning brightly in your marriage. For some additional ideas, see the "Baker's Dozen" ideas at the end of this chapter. But do more than read these ideas. Use some of them regularly, and your account in your spouse's Love Bank will grow into a nice IRA!

COMMUNICATION BUILDS COUPLE POWER

In today's busy society *communication* is an overused word and an underdeveloped skill. I find this to be especially true on the part of husbands. There is no question that one of a woman's five basic needs is for communication—and that means communicating about more than "What's for dinner?" or "Want to watch CNN or a rerun of *Cheers*?" When a husband doesn't try to communicate with his wife he is setting her up to be drawn into an affair with a man who is *willing to talk—and to listen.*

Frequently, when women tell me about marital problems, I can sense that there has been infidelity on somebody's part. Finally, I may ask, "Have you engaged in any affairs?"

At that point I get "the look" that tells me more than any of her words could say. But when she goes on to describe her affair, it is often a story not of passionate, nonstop sex, but of caring, conversation, and communicating. In many cases her eyes will drop slightly and then she'll look up and say, "I suppose you won't believe me, but we've been together now for six months, and there hasn't been any sex."

She's quite sure I won't understand, but I do understand because I know that there is a one-to-one correlation between an extramarital affair and a void in a marriage. She has found someone who will listen to her, talk to her, share feelings with her, and be excited over the little things in life with her.

Obviously this wasn't happening at all at home. As I've already said, the only good thing you can say about an affair is that it tells you exactly what's wrong in a marriage.

That's why I'm convinced there are many kinds of affairs. Yes, there are the torrid sexual marathons, where the straying mate and the lover can't get enough of each other physically. At the other end of the spectrum, there are liaisons where an unhappy mate finds someone who will just listen to her for hours, sometimes long distance on the phone. She will say, "What feels so right about it is that I can just tell him anything. I don't feel as if I have to measure up, jump higher, or do anything but be myself."

In other cases, it's a combination of sex and communicating. She will say, "Yes, we've had sex, but that isn't really it. There are so many other things, like the time we went for a walk by this lovely stream to a waterfall, and we stood together underneath the falls, getting soaked and just laughing and enjoying each other. And there was the time we just lay on the leaves together and looked up through the trees at the sky. I never felt like doing any of that with my husband. Why do I feel like doing it with him?"

The answer is simple. He listens, he takes time, he's gentle, he's interested in *her.* For the woman who craves intimacy, I advise marrying a man who enjoys lying on the leaves on a warm autumn day and gazing up at the blue sky. When a man has that kind of sensitivity, warmth, and spontaneity, the intimacy connection is much easier to maintain.

For husbands and wives who want to work on communication, I suggest two approaches, which are exactly 180 degrees apart in strategy. The first approach is designed particularly for wives who have the notorious "Harry the Turtle" for a husband. No matter how much they nag, no matter how much they beg him to talk, he just seems to go deeper into his shell.

In severe cases of this kind, I sometimes advise the wife, "Don't say anything." In other words, quit nagging, quit pounding on the shell, quit demanding that he come out to play or at least to talk. In other words, wait him out by backing off and not asking so many questions.

When you ask question after question, you only succeed in putting Harry on the defensive. Even the most innocuous question, such as, "How was your day today, honey?" can irritate him. Instead, work at making statements instead of phrasing questions, because questions always encourage the same deadly routine:

"How was your day?" she asks.

"Fine," he grunts, and the conversation dies a quiet death.

When Harry the Turtle thinks he sees his wife coming with her long list of questions and pry bar in hand, he simply retreats into his shell until she goes away.

But suppose a couple is eating dinner, and the wife is dying to know how a big meeting went at work. Instead of asking, "Harry, I'm dying to know, how did it go with your boss today?" she should try a simple command: "Tell me about the meeting." Believe it or not, with Harry the Turtle, gentle commands go down much easier than questions. "Tell me about . . ." is open-ended and not as threatening as a direct question.

SHOULDS AND OUGHTS ARE DEADLY

At the other end of the spectrum is the approach of fanning any flicker of conversation into something resembling communication. One of the big mistakes many couples make is that when a tiny flame of communication does spring up, they manage to douse it immediately with a big bucket of *shoulds* and *oughts*. It's not a very original observation, but it's still all too true: People don't like to be told what to do. And that goes double for your spouse.

Along with the *shoulds* and *oughts,* husbands and wives are very good at saying *always* and *never.* If there is anything we can say about the use of such absolutes, it is this: *Absolutely never* use them!

Here are some other tips about how to communicate. They apply equally to husbands and wives, but admittedly, husbands may profit more from using even one of these ideas to rebuild the intimacy connection.

Deliberately plan for some time together. Examine your typical schedules, and pick times when you can focus on each other's feelings, concerns, and interests. This could be at dinner, but it may work better just before going to sleep. Try lying in each other's arms and talking about how you feel—what is causing joy, what is causing anxiety and concern. Make it a time to be open and honest, but avoid attacking and complaining.

As one mate talks, the other should listen. Books have been written about the need for couples to listen to each other, and what these books say is true. The trouble is, few people know how to listen, and perhaps even fewer want to listen. It's a human weakness to want to think about what you are going to say next in a conversation rather than listen to a person who is trying to say something to you.

Try sitting comfortably facing each other. Choose a subject—something a little more intimate than the weather—and let one spouse—the wife, for example—begin telling her husband how she feels about this subject. The husband is not to interrupt but only to listen. When his wife stops talking, he must share back what he believes she said. Then his wife can either affirm, deny, or modify what she meant and what he heard.

Then the partners should switch roles and let the wife listen and feed back what she thinks she heard her husband say.

Admittedly, this little exercise is artificial and "unnatural," but if you are having trouble communicating, it's a great first step toward better conversations in the future. What you are learning is the art of listening—really hearing what your mate is trying to say.

Don't talk to your mate to try to change him or her. Communicate with one purpose in mind: To learn how to be a better marriage partner. Stay away from should-ing, ought-ing, always-ing, and never-ing each other. I like the way Willard Harley puts it: "An intimate conversation cannot include an argument."[5]

KIDNAP HIM AND COMMUNICATE

The ideas I've just presented are nothing new. You can find them along with many others in any marriage manual or book on communication. The important thing is to determine together that you *want* to try to communicate. I realize that many wives reading this will say, "But that's just the point—he doesn't want to communicate. How do I get his attention? How do I let him know my ideas have merit?"

One approach I've suggested that has worked for many wives revolves around "kidnapping" the husband—either for a weekend or even for a night out to dinner. I don't care how you arrange it, but get him into a situation where you can say, "You may not think what I'm going to say is important, but I want you to know that I'd really like to do more of this with you, but something keeps stopping me and I want to explain what that is."

Then the wife can share her feelings—quietly, lovingly, without using *should, ought, never,* or *always.* Yes, I realize some husbands will not listen and that some will possibly even become angry. But if your Love Bank is growing empty and the intimacy connection is frayed, if not broken, what do you have to lose? On the other hand, it's just possible that he may listen. I know of many husbands who have listened and who are now taking tiny baby steps toward reconnecting with their wives on an intimate basis.

WHAT DOES YOUR MATE
REALLY WANT YOU TO DO?

One of the best conversations Sande and I ever had happened a few years ago, when I decided to solicit her ideas on how I could be a better husband. I asked her to name at least ten things that she really appreciates and wants me to do regularly. Here is what she told me:

1. Whenever I'm sick, take the kids to church anyway.
2. I like it when you scratch and rub my back to wake me up in the mornings—and bring me coffee.
3. I like it when you help with the dishes and picking up around the house, when you see what needs to be taken care of and you take care of it and I don't have to point it out.
4. I also like it when you don't call attention to what you're doing to help. Rattling the empty coffee cups to let me know you're taking them to the sink doesn't impress me.
5. I love it when you say, "You need a weekend away. I've made arrangements for you to spend some time alone." Along with that, I want you to take care of the kids, not just dump them off at my mother's.
6. Oh, yes, I also really appreciate what you do for my mother, like providing her with transportation and helping her get things fixed around the house.
7. I like it when you take my car out to be washed and serviced—and then I'm sure it's safe to drive.
8. You don't know how much I appreciate it on those days I'm at the end of my rope with the children and you take over when they really get wild and start arguing with each other.
9. I like it when you make the plans for us to go out. You get the baby-sitter, you call up our friends and set a time to meet them—everything isn't left for me.

10. And, finally, I love it when you're patient and understanding—especially if I've had a bad day. Like the time you came home after I drove the car through the garage door. You had to have seen the door when you drove up, but you walked in and said, "Honey, how was your day?" I said, "Oh, *fine!*" and I was almost ready to cry when you said, "Let's go out to dinner."

Obviously, any wife or husband would have a different list of ten things they appreciate having their spouse do or say. Try exchanging your own lists soon. You will probably learn a great deal—about needs you are meeting and about some you are not. You will also get ideas about how to do better Love Banking and build stronger intimacy connections. And while you're at it, you will be affair-proofing your marriage, because you'll be putting your marriage first—where it always belongs.

DON'T FORGET . . .

- Extramarital affairs are almost always the tragic result of unmet needs in a marriage.
- Marital intimacy often dies of sheer neglect.
- To affair-proof your marriage, avoid temptation, rekindle romance, and develop couple power.
- Always stay out of situations where you may be overmatched or tempted beyond your limits.
- Admit that you can't always handle certain situations or temptations.
- Satisfied partners don't wander.
- Romance improves in most marriages when the wife becomes more sexually aggressive and the man becomes more patient and gentle.
- *Shoulds, oughts,* and banal questions often kill communication.

A BAKER'S DOZEN WAYS TO
FILL HER LOVE BANK

1. Treat her as important. Let her know that you want to understand how she feels.
2. Ask her opinions. Don't surprise her with arbitrary, unilateral decisions.
3. Give her frequent hugs, especially if she is feeling down or depressed. Just hold her, no lectures or advice.
4. Talk to her about how she spends her day—at work or at home. Be *interested*.
5. Always handle her with care in every way.
6. Accept her as she is; change yourself, not her.
7. Get rid of habits that annoy her.
8. When you help around the house, don't expect a twenty-one-gun salute.
9. Let her know how proud you are that she is your wife.
10. Call if you're going to be late.
11. Besides remembering birthdays, anniversaries, and holidays, surprise her with a card or some flowers for no special reason except that you love her.
12. When she shares a problem with you, don't immediately jump in to be The Great Fixer. Chances are she knows how to solve the problem already and just wants you to listen and empathize.
13. *Never* give her a toaster on any special occasion, not even a four-slicer. And that goes double for frying pans, waffle irons, and can openers.

A BAKER'S DOZEN WAYS TO
FILL HIS LOVE BANK

1. Admire his achievements; let him know you're aware of the stress he's under at work.
2. Keep your "honey-do" list down to a reasonable number of items. Show him special thanks when he takes care of something on the list.
3. Don't second-guess him in front of the kids. Disagree in private.
4. Ask him how you could be more sexually aggressive.
5. Handle his "male ego" with care. Always try to preserve his self-esteem.
6. Accept him as he is; change yourself, not him.
7. Get rid of habits that annoy him.
8. Make it a point to pay special attention to him rather than always centering on the children.
9. Thank him for his contributions to the family without adding, "Only I wish . . ."
10. Call if you're going to be late.
11. If you give him something to read, don't bug him about it.
12. Instead of always waiting for him to remember your anniversary, kidnap him and take him on a special anniversary dinner or weekend yourself.
13. If your husband is the "Harry the Turtle" type, try not asking him any questions for a week.

Chapter Ten

NEGOTIATE A MUTUALLY SATISFYING SEXUAL RELATIONSHIP*

Dr. Neil Clark Warren

One of the most comprehensive sex surveys ever conducted in the United States contains one shocking statistic after another. Published a few years ago, the results of this survey are so incompatible with what we thought to be true about the sexual behavior of Americans that we can celebrate with happy surprise.

This survey was conducted by a team of highly qualified researchers from the University of Chicago, and 3,342 respondents were each thoroughly interviewed about his or her sexual history. Every part of the study received excruciatingly thoughtful attention, and the results seem unusually trustworthy.

Here are ten findings from the study that strike me as particularly critical to our thinking:

1. This study found that monogamous couples are significantly happier in their sexual relationships. What a surprise for many people in our society!
2. The data indicate that 80 percent of married people receive great physical pleasure from their sexual relationships, and 85 percent reported the same positive experience in the emotional area. Who ever said that marital sex is bland?

*Adapted from *The Triumphant Marriage* by Neil Clark Warren, Ph.D., a Focus on the Family book published by Tyndale House. Copyright © 1995 by Neil Clark Warren, Ph.D. All rights reserved. International copyright secured. Used by permission.

3. There was a strong consensus that extramarital sex is wrong. And 94 percent of all married persons in the survey had only one sexual partner—their spouse—in the last year.

4. A satisfying sex life is not totally dependent on having orgasms. While only 29 percent of women reported always having orgasms during sex compared to 75 percent of men, the percentage of women and men who find their sex life "extremely" physically and emotionally satisfying is about the same—40 percent.

5. An overwhelming number of Americans are unusually traditional in their sexual habits. For instance, 95 percent of all respondents said they had vaginal intercourse the last time they had sex, and 85 percent said that was the case every time they had sex in the past year. All the talk about a wide variety of sexual predilections of Americans seems totally inaccurate. We are not a nation of people that seeks sexual variety.

6. The study strongly refutes the notion that everyone in the United States is equally at risk for AIDS. The general population simply does not have continuing sexual or needle-sharing contact with the two social groups in which AIDS is most prevalent—gay men living in large cities and intravenous drug users and their partners.

7. However, one in six survey respondents reported having had a sexually transmitted disease at some point. More women than men had been infected, and persons who had engaged in unprotected sex with multiple partners were far more likely to have had such a disease.

8. Twelve percent of the men in the survey and 17 percent of the women reported having been sexually touched by someone older when they were twelve years old or younger. These persons also reported higher levels of sexual dysfunction and general unhappiness.

9. Only 1.4 percent of women and 2.8 percent of men in the survey identified themselves as homosexual or bisexual.

10. The averages for frequency and duration of sex for married couples are amazingly consistent across racial, religious, and educational groups. Both frequency and duration are affected by the age level of the participants, with an average frequency range for number of sexual encounters per month running from four to eight, and an average time duration for each sexual experience running from fifteen minutes to more than an hour.[1]

THE IMPORTANCE OF SEXUALITY IN MARRIAGE

Wanting to learn what leads to an extremely happy and healthy marriage, I wrote to friends and colleagues all over the country and asked them to nominate the healthiest marriage they know. I ended up with two hundred spouses in one hundred extremely healthy marriages, and I asked them everything I could think of about how they have become so successful—including questions about their sexual relationship. Their responses covered a broad range of sexual satisfaction. One man said, "Our sexual relationship has been good, but not fully satisfactory. It was best early in our marriage, then not as satisfactory for many years, and now is better again. Sex is not the most important thing in our marriage." Another man said, "I had anticipated our sexual relationship to be a huge part of our marriage. It is important, but not nearly as important as I expected, and far less important than many other things." It seems clear that some highly successful marriages do not include a sexual component that is totally satisfying.

Other persons talked about improvement in sexual satisfaction over the course of their marriage and the many benefits that accrue from this change. One lady said, "We were both somewhat inhibited initially, and it was some time before I was able to communicate my needs. Our sexual relationship is great now—and a very important part of our marriage."

While it seems clear that a mutually satisfying sexual relationship enhances every marriage, it is equally clear that great marriages can often be fashioned without great sex. But there's little doubt that if great sex for both partners can be obtained, it will contribute substantially to the management of marital stress and the attainment of marital goals.

Dr. Clifford and Joyce Penner have been my partners in the practice of psychology for nearly twenty-five years. They have written six excellent books about sexual adjustment in marriage, the most famous being the best-selling *The Gift of Sex*.[2] I interviewed them for several hours in preparation for writing this chapter. I began with this question: "What percentage of couples can attain a mutually satisfying sexual relationship?" I was startled when they both answered at the same time with the same answer: "100 percent of them." When I pressed them, Cliff said, "We've never worked with a single married couple whom we felt were incapable of attaining a high level of sexual satisfaction with each other."

"Amazing!" I said. "How many of these couples attain this kind of mutual satisfaction quite naturally, without having to really work at it?"

"About one-third of them," Joyce replied.

Over the next few hours, I asked the Penners every question I could think of about how the "other two-thirds" of all married couples can reach the high level of sexual satisfaction that so greatly facilitates the building of a triumphant marriage. Their answers were straightforward, clear, and simple.

TEN CRUCIAL FACTORS FOR A GREAT SEX LIFE

I asked the Penners for their list of recommendations for any couple who wants to have a mutually satisfying sexual relationship. After twenty-five years of holding seminars throughout North America, working with thousands of couples on their sexual relationship, appearing on hundreds of radio and television talk shows, and writing all these books about great sex in marriage, the Penners came at my question with tremendous enthusiasm and confidence. Here are the ten recommendations they have for how to create a great sex life:

1. *The most vital factor in producing a great sexual relationship in marriage revolves around the role of the man.* The Penners have found that sexual patterns in a marriage begin to change dramatically when the man changes, even when the woman may be the one hindering a vital sexual relationship. So even though "it takes two to tango," as they say, the greater responsibility for improvement rests with the husband.

2. *The man must move in the direction of the woman's needs.* He needs to become acutely aware of as many of her spiritual and emotional needs as he possibly can. His awareness, obviously, will increase in direct proportion to his ability to listen to her.

3. *The woman needs to learn how to take.* She needs to listen carefully to her body and then seek what will satisfy her desires. Though wives are typically eager to please their husbands, they should be ready to receive an equal degree of pleasure.

4. *The woman must feel free to lead in the sexual experience.* The Penners quoted an Old Testament passage from the Song of Songs that teaches a three-step process that leads to dramatic sexual improvement.

First, the man affirms the woman; he talks freely about her virtues. Second, the woman takes the lead; she proceeds at her speed, and she lets the man know her thoughts and desires at all times. Third, the man responds; he listens carefully to what she says, and he acts only in response to her desires. (The most common example is that women stop kissing passionately because the man always wants more. If women want to kiss for an hour and that's all, men should accommodate that wish.)

5. *The man must progress very s-l-o-w-l-y.* The previous point was so important that the Penners underlined it by saying, "The man must slow way down." They referred to the song by the Pointer Sisters about the man with the "slow hand." The image that represents the best relative pace for the two persons involves a man and woman riding their separate bicycles down the road. The woman is slightly in the lead, and the man rides with his front wheel just behind her front wheel. He isn't far behind, but he lets her take the lead.

6. *The man needs to remain flexible, without a set "agenda" for how things are supposed to go.* His "guidance system" should be his wife. Many men try to get the recipe down and then follow it. This almost never works because a woman's sexual desires, needs, and responses cannot be predicted from one time to the next.

7. *Both husband and wife need to be into the sexual process for the pleasure of it—not for the result of it.* The goal of sex is to build intimacy with your spouse. The secret is to enjoy both your own body and your partner's. If climax is not reached for either partner, it shouldn't be seen as a big disappointment or failure.

8. *If one of the partners was the victim of sexual abuse during childhood, there must be healing from the trauma.* The victims of abuse often carry into marriage emotional scars that hinder free and uninhibited sexual expression. (And understand that they are the victims. I have the utmost compassion for those who have suffered abuse.) Most often this healing process requires a professional to help you face the abuse, grieve the losses involved, and regain a sense of wholeness. In addition, support groups and books are readily available to help you through this process. (The University of Chicago study stated that 17 percent of women are abused during childhood. However, after years of clinical research, the Penners believe that number is actually closer to 35 percent.)

9. *Mutual satisfaction is the expectation in every sexual experience.* The woman must be able to allow an orgasm if she wants

one. The fundamental requirement for satisfaction, however, is a deep sense of interpersonal closeness and warmth.

10. *It is vital that both partners know how the body works sexually.* Don't laugh! Most people enter marriage with many misconceptions about how things work. A thorough understanding will make expectations far more reasonable, and couples won't suffer from the disappointment and disillusionment that come from unrealistic desires and demands.

I want to make it clear that mutual sexual satisfaction is a goal that every couple should pursue with great enthusiasm. If all couples in North America could spend a few hours with highly competent sexual therapists like the Penners, their marriages would experience a dramatic improvement in this area. If you need guidance along the way to help make your sex life deeply satisfying, I encourage you to look for professionals who are emotionally healthy themselves, and who have the ability to help couples merge physical technique and spiritual sensitivity into a totally delightful sexual experience. If there are no sexual counselors in your area, I encourage you to buy a good book on marital sex, read it with your spouse, and keep working on the development of your sexual relationship.

SEXUAL SATISFACTION AS AN INDEX OF RELATIONAL HEALTH

My clinical experience has taught me that the relationship between marital health and sexual satisfaction is a very complex one. For instance, I have worked with some couples whose overall compatibility ratio is very low, but their sexual satisfaction level is unusually high. I have had some couples who simply couldn't get along, and they separated, but they continued seeing each other frequently to have sex. I have worked with other couples who virtually hated each other, but they didn't separate because they couldn't imagine giving up something as vital to them as their sexual relationship. One couple actually told me that they both keep their eyes tightly closed during sex because, as good as the sex is, they can't stand even the thought of being with each other, let alone making love to each other.

On the other hand, I have seen scores of couples through the years who felt they didn't have a very satisfying sexual relationship but loved each other deeply. Many of these couples would never consider leaving the marriage; in fact, they might very well rate their marriage as extremely satisfying.

There is little doubt in my mind that when all other factors are positive for a couple, the lack of a good sexual relationship will seldom sink the image. Sex is usually not vital enough to devastate any marriage all by itself—if other factors are sufficiently positive. But I must tell you that I have never seen what I call a triumphant marriage in which the sexual relationship was disappointing. And even though I mentioned earlier about the way that some couples stay together (or get together periodically) for the sex even though their relationship is worse than mediocre, the fact is that a great sexual relationship enhances most marriages in a significant way.

I believe that if we could teach every couple in North America to improve their sexual relationship by just ten percent, we could lower the divorce rate by more than ten percent. Further, we could increase the marital satisfaction rate enormously. Why? Because every couple in America would suddenly have a sexual relationship that's ten percent better, and even more important, every couple would have a sense of hope. It's hope that brings about an acceleration of marital growth. The hope rests on the fact that if we can get a ten-percent improvement rate for every couple, then why can't we get a fifteen-percent improvement rate? When improvement becomes possible on the basis of factors over which we have control, we begin to sense that there may be incredible gains available to those couples who want to work hard at it.

SEXUAL PROBLEMS IN MARRIAGE: THREE CASE STUDIES

In order to illustrate the various types of sexual problems in marriage and how to proceed with them, I want to tell you about three actual cases.

Case Study #1: Laurel and Steve

Laurel, a twenty-nine-year-old mother of two sons, called me about her marriage. She and Steve, thirty-two, had been married seven years and had tried two other counselors, but Steve always found an excuse for not attending after a couple of sessions. I set up an appointment to see them the next day.

They came together, and I escorted them in from the waiting room right on time. Laurel was eager to talk, and she would have dominated the conversation if I hadn't continued to make plenty of conversational space for Steve. What became obvious early on was that Laurel was filled with concern about her marriage. She was frightened that it was falling apart, and she felt totally helpless to change it. The more her anxiety motivated her to talk, the more Steve—like a turtle—pulled his head in under his thick shell.

I perceived that Laurel was reasonably happy, stable, and emotionally secure. The problems didn't seem to belong to her. The only thing I needed to do with her was to calm her down and get her to back off. She kept us from focusing squarely on Steve's problem because her nervous chatter kept getting in the way.

The superficial description of their problem went like this: The relationship seemed fine during the courtship and for the first two years of marriage, but after their first son was born, sex between them became more and more infrequent and unsatisfying. Their current sexual relationship was almost nonexistent. From Laurel's point of view, Steve had totally withdrawn from her. When this withdrawal had started several years earlier, Laurel had tried everything. For several months, she attempted to reason with him, but this usually led to even greater distancing. Then she tried to woo him with flashier clothes, carefully planned meals, and weekends away. Despite her efforts, nothing seemed to draw Steve back into the relationship.

I suggested individual appointments early in the next week. I was especially interested in seeing Steve, because I had become more and more convinced that the problem was with him.

I'm certainly not always right, but this time I was. The hour with Steve was filled with stories about his early life that moved like a heat-seeking missile to his relationship with his stepfather. In one of those heartbreaking revelations, he told me how his stepfather had sexually violated him when Steve was only eleven years old. The abuse had continued for four years, and every time Steve was in the house and his mother was at work, Steve became vulnerable to this man's pathological domination.

"Have you ever shared this with Laurel?" I asked.

"No."

"May I ask you why not?"

Staring at the floor, he replied quietly that he was too ashamed.

I then asked, "What about the two other therapists you saw? Did you tell them?"

"No," he said. "I never saw them alone. I was always with Laurel."

He did say, though, that he desperately wanted to deal with the issue, because he saw how it was damaging his marriage. Nevertheless, he still wasn't ready to tell Laurel about it.

"Okay," I said. "I want to see you twice a week so that we can get to work on this severe psychic injury." Steve agreed in an instant. I worked it out with Laurel so that I could see Steve alone without raising her suspicion too much.

He never missed a session, and he was not late once. His sexual problems persisted, but in time we worked through the hurt, fear, guilt, shame, and sexual-identity confusion he experienced. After several months, we brought Laurel in, and Steve was able to tell her everything. While our progress was something like two-steps-forward-one-step-back, it was positive enough that within a few months, Steve and Laurel began feeling substantially closer to each other. Little gains turned into slightly bigger ones, and eventually, they were far along the road to recovery.

Sometimes, in cases like this one, the sexual problem is not a marital problem at all. In a world in which children are often victims of horrible crimes, the result is frequently a kind of brokenness that shows itself wherever relational intimacy is most intense. What we have to guard against in cases like this one is that the marriage doesn't get blamed.

There was no way that Steve and Laurel could ever have had a decent sexual relationship until Steve had a chance to heal. Laurel's nature was to confront the problem, to take the blame if she needed to, and to take as much control of the situation as she could. All her efforts in this regard only made things worse. The more she pursued Steve, the more he ran away to protect his secret. Thank God for the individual time I had with Steve that allowed him to share the truth. This lit the path we needed to follow to help him recover—and to give his marriage a wonderful future.

Case Study #2: Jim and Erin

Jim told me during our first session that "his marriage had gone flat." Nothing was seriously wrong, but nothing was right either. Sex for him and Erin was infrequent, and he was frustrated by how blasé their marriage had become.

When I saw them together for the first time, Jim did seventy-five percent of the talking. Erin spoke only when I asked her a question. I immediately liked what I could see of Erin, but I found Jim overly smooth, overly confident, overly critical, and exceptionally elusive to my psychological "scanner." It seemed to me that I wasn't seeing the real Jim, that maybe he was hiding something. When I saw them individually at subsequent sessions, I tried to remedy the earlier situation. I fed Erin a lot of questions and gave her plenty of room to talk. She did! I heard all about a marriage that was lived in the shadow of Jim's big, successful, dominating family—a family that was rich and well educated and unusually sure of itself.

With Jim, I tried to get him off of his ice skates. That is, I wanted to keep him from skating away from me, from smoothly avoiding each of my questions. He was trying to get my help in bringing Erin into line without letting me see his role in the problem.

Here is what I began to discover from those individual sessions. Erin had traded her individuality and uniqueness for the status and security of Jim's money and confidence. She had come from a poor family, and Jim represented a way out. What she didn't know was that while Jim's family had an abundance of money, they had a serious lack of emotional health. Jim was confident all right—far too confident. He was too wrapped up in himself, too well defended, too unconsciously fragile. He suffered from an emotional problem called narcissistic personality disturbance. In other words, his needs completely dominated his life; they overshadowed Erin and their marriage. There was going to be no good marriage and no good sexual relationship until Jim addressed his internal fragility.

I must tell you that I was, sadly, unable to help Jim. He had a very hard time seeing that he was a source of any of the marital problems. It was obvious to him that Erin was the reason their sex was poor, and that if she would shape up, the sex and the marriage would improve. He came to me reluctantly for a short period, kept his distance from me, and tried desperately to help me see that Erin was the real problem. He was fortified within his emotional defense system. He suffered from a pervasive fear that if he ever began to soften, he might have to change his life dramatically. He badly needed to "die to this old self" so that he could build a healthy self-conception, but he refused to surrender.

There was no way Erin was ever going to trust Jim with her body—let alone her soul. He was so tied up in his frantic efforts to love himself that he had little, if any, real love for her. Erin's self-esteem was low, and she suffered from a mild form of depression. The fact was that she was trapped in a marriage that called for her to give up her personhood. Fortunately, she was too healthy to do that.

The bottom line is this: Sometimes sexual difficulties are the consequence of a marital system that has gone bad because one person is emotionally ill. Until this illness is addressed, the sex probably won't get much better. If the sex does get better without any improvement of the real problems, it is not likely to last for long. Sexual health proceeds out of the most sacred inner places for two persons, and it is not likely to be healthy for long unless the partners become genuinely healthy.

Case Study #3: Jane and Mark

Jane and Mark had been married for two years when they came to see me. It was clear they were deeply in love, but they were terribly frustrated with their marriage.

They told me a sad story. Jane came from a divorced home, and from the time she was nine years old she saw her dad only three or four times a year. Even when she was seven or eight years old, Jane knew that her dad was involved with other women. She agonized for her mom, whom Jane saw as an innocent victim. Jane had terribly mixed feelings about her dad. She yearned for him to like her, to want to be with her, but he had married another woman, moved to the East Coast, and he had two children with his new wife. He had little time for Jane, and even when they did get together, he seemed preoccupied and ill at ease. Jane suspected that he was involved with other women again.

That deeply painful experience with her father had poisoned Jane's trust of others. And she failed to differentiate between her dad and Mark. If Mark was five minutes late coming home from work, she suspected him. If he was out of the office during the day when she called, she was sure he was with some other woman. Her fears and imagination were running wild. But through all of this, she was ashamed to tell Mark how seriously and frequently she doubted him.

All of this mistrust came out in their sexual relationship. How could she ever give herself to someone she so deeply suspected of violating her? She couldn't! So she went to bed long before he did and often feigned that she was asleep when he came to bed. She had physical illnesses of one kind or another whenever he tried to initiate sex. She had even started sleeping in a different bedroom at times, telling Mark that his snoring kept her awake.

When I discovered what the real issue was, we went to work on Jane's suspicions, her deep and pervasive doubts about the integrity of her husband. This case turned out just the way we hoped and prayed it would. Jane became consciously clear about the extreme differences in the character of her father and her husband. She took control of her unconscious transference. She began to program herself to think twice before she let her suspicions about her father control her perception of her husband. In time, she and Mark developed a trusting relationship, and with some coaching and cheerleading from me, their sex life became thoroughly satisfying to both of them.

CASES I REFER TO OTHER PROFESSIONALS

Obviously, there are all kinds of reasons for sexual problems. I've told you about three of these, but there are many others. Certain problems I like to refer to people who specialize in sexual therapy. For instance, if a man is impotent, I like to have my colleagues, the Penners, cooperate with his urologist in finding a cure for his impotence. The same is true of premature ejaculation for a man and vaginismus for a woman (a condition in which the vagina remains too tight for penis penetration). Most of these cases can be cured efficiently, but they require a considerable amount of technical expertise.

Nevertheless, the vast majority of sexual problems result from psychological factors, and these issues must be carefully addressed before the sexual relationship is likely to improve. There is no better feeling for a psychotherapist than the elation that comes from a careful management of psychological problems—and a sexual relationship that becomes wonderfully satisfying.

THE CRITICAL CONTRIBUTION
OF A SPIRITUAL BOND

The best sexual relationship is one that proceeds out of a couple's deep and intimate "soul bonding." Show me a couple for whom feelings and thoughts are shared from the innermost levels, and I'll show you a couple ready to have a triumphant sexual relationship. If their sexual relationship is not triumphant, they probably only need some careful instruction and coaching.

It is spiritual bonding that characterizes the finest marital relationships. Spiritual bonding comes from hard work that is carried out in an atmosphere of deep trust. When spiritual bonding is established, sex is a lot more than the merging of body parts. What really happens is that the souls of two people get woven together. This is even more important than orgasm, but orgasm is likely to happen when the spiritual bond develops. This is when euphoria is experienced!

A FIVE-STEP PLAN FOR A TEN-PERCENT GAIN

Marriages in North America would be enormously enhanced if couples could experience a ten-percent gain in the mutual satisfaction level of their sexual relationship. I am totally confident that couples *can* experience this ten-percent improvement in their sexual relationship within the next six months. The plan is straightforward, but it does require some regular collaboration of both spouses.

1. *You both must be willing to try.* If you can say to each other that you would like to take this challenge together and that you're willing to work on it over the next six months, you have completed the first of five simple steps. Reminder: As a couple, you are not trying for perfection in the sexual area of your relationship. You may not be trying for anything close to perfection! You're simply trying to improve your sexual relationship by ten percent over a six-month period, and you're committed to working through this five-step plan. Whatever you do, don't put yourself under the stress of unrealistic expectations. Figure out what a ten-percent improvement would be for the two of you, and then get about the job of doing these five things.

2. *Buy a good book on marital sex.* I recommend *Restoring the Pleasure* by Clifford and Joyce Penner.[3] Make an agreement with each other to read a chapter (preferably out loud) three times a week. Read each chapter fully, and take time to discuss any exercises that are recommended. When you finish this, you have completed step two, and you are well on your way to improving your sexual relationship by ten percent.

3. *If either of you experienced sexual abuse in your childhood, immediately begin processing the trauma.* Select a competent and

caring professional in your area—or join a counseling group—to help you experience wholeness as completely and thoroughly as possible.

4. *Husbands, practice taking an affirming and responsive role in the sexual relationship.* Start listening to your wife both emotionally and spiritually. Ask her questions about herself, and then listen, listen, listen. Practice the various suggestions the Penners made earlier: (a) affirm your wife, let her take the lead, and then respond to her; (b) proceed slowly; (c) allow her to guide the process, but follow close behind; (d) be into the sexual process for the pleasure of it, rather than for the result of it.

5. *Learn to talk freely as a couple about your sexual feelings.* Many couples find it awkward and embarrassing to talk about their sexual needs. But relying on guesswork usually isn't very helpful. Work hard at being completely open about your sexual needs, and work even harder at understanding what the other person's needs are. Encourage each other to take initiative in the sexual process, but make sure that both of you wish to proceed before you get further involved.

If you and your spouse will follow this simple plan for six months, I strongly suspect that your sexual relationship will be a full ten percent better. If it is, you have done something together of gigantic importance for the future of your marriage. The secret is to keep working at this for six months. Persistence and the right attitude will bring dramatic results.

How much hope is there for the sexual relationship in your marriage? All kinds! If you will follow this five-step program, I am totally confident that your sexual relationship can grow by leaps and bounds. Follow these five steps faithfully for six months, and see if your sexual relationship isn't ten percent better. If it is, what might another six months of dedicated work mean for the two of you?

Chapter Eleven

WHAT NO WOMAN CAN RESIST*
Gary Smalley

The crunch of corn chips distracted my attention from the Saturday afternoon football game. I watched in amazement as my wife and three children began to eat their sandwiches and drink their Cokes while I sat only a couple of feet away without a bite to eat.

Why didn't she make me a sandwich? I asked myself. *I'm the sole breadwinner, and I'm being ignored as if I didn't exist.* I cleared my throat loudly to catch my wife's attention. When that didn't work, I became so irritated that I walked into the kitchen, got the bread out, and made my own sandwich. When I sat back down in front of the TV, Norma didn't say a word; nor did I. But I kept wondering, *If women are so sensitive, how come she didn't know I wanted a sandwich? If women are so alert, why didn't she hear me clear my throat or notice that I wasn't speaking to her? Why didn't she notice the expression of irritation on my face?*

A few days later when we were talking calmly, I said, "I've really been wondering about something, but I hesitate asking you this question. I was really intrigued the other day, and I wonder if I could ask you a personal question?" By now I had aroused her curiosity.

"Sure," she said.

"You know last Saturday when I was watching the football game and you made sandwiches for all the kids? Could I ask you why you didn't make one for me?"

---

*Adapted from *Hidden Keys of a Loving, Lasting Marriage* by Gary Smalley. Copyright © 1984, 1988. Used by permission.

"Are you serious?" she asked. She looked at me with such amazement that it really confused me.

"Sure, I'm serious. I would think that since I'm the one who earns all the money for food around here that you would have made me something to eat too."

"You know, I really can't believe that you would even ask a question like that," she said. By now, I was thinking, *Maybe I shouldn't have asked. Maybe I should know the answer.* It seemed very obvious to her, but it didn't seem obvious to me at all.

"Norma, I really don't see it. I admit I am blind in some areas," I pursued, "and I can see this is one of them. Would you mind telling me?"

"Sometimes women are accused of being stupid, but we aren't," she answered. "We don't just set ourselves up to be criticized." She seemed to think that explained why she hadn't made me a sandwich.

"I can understand that. But what does that have to do with the sandwiches?"

"Do you realize that every time I make you a sandwich, you say something critical about it? 'Norma, you didn't give me enough lettuce . . . Is this avocado ripe? You put too much mayonnaise on this. Hey, how about some butter? Well, it's a little dry . . .'

"Maybe you've never realized it, but you have had a critical statement for every sandwich I ever made. I just wasn't up to being criticized the other day. It wasn't worth it. I don't enjoy being criticized."

I had egg all over my face because I could recall many times when I had criticized her as she handed me sandwiches. But "every" time? I wanted to say, "Come on, Norma, let's get realistic! Every time?" But instead I remembered that for a woman, "always" and "never" don't mean the same thing as they do to a man when they're spoken with emotion. Norma's tone of voice and facial expression as well as her words were telling me this was something that really bothered her. I was simply eating the fruit of my ways. I sowed criticism and reaped an empty plate. I am happy to say that after that experience I began praising every sandwich she made for me, and now she unhesitatingly makes them for me.

Shortly after Marilyn left Bob, I asked her if she could recall things for which Bob had praised her. She couldn't remember a single time during their twenty-plus years of marriage. Her children confirmed it. They agreed that their mother had never served a single dinner that their father didn't criticize in at least one way. He had complained when the salt and pepper weren't on the table or when she didn't cook the meat just right. She finally reached the point where she didn't even want to be near his critical personality. She left him for another man.

"I'm kind of happy she's leaving me, because she never wants to do anything with me anyway," Bob said. "She's a party pooper and a loner. She excludes me from her activities. Do you know she never wanted to go on a vacation with me? I've tried and I've tried, but she never wants to. I'm disgusted with her too."

We didn't discuss his marital problems until after he told me about his job change due to friction with his former boss.

"How did he treat you, Bob?" I asked.

"He'd come out to the shop where I was the foreman, and he'd look for one little thing to yell at me about in front of all my men. That really hurt me deeply. Then he would go back to his office, and I'd continue working my fingers to the bone. He'd never notice how hard I worked or even say anything positive about it. I couldn't take it anymore, so I asked for a transfer."

I asked Bob, "Would you take a vacation with your boss?"

"Are you kidding? That would be the worst thing in the world," he answered.

"How about doing other activities with him?"

"No way! He's so critical he'd even ruin a trip to Hawaii!"

What I told Bob next blew open his mind to finally understand his wife. I pointed out how as a husband he was just like his
boss, and his face dropped and tears came to his eyes.

"You're right. No wonder Marilyn never wanted to go anywhere
with me. I never think about things she does to please me, and I'm
always criticizing her in front of the children and our friends."

But it was too late. Marilyn was already in love with another
man. Though Bob changed drastically and is now much more sensitive to women, his wife divorced him and remarried.

Women need praise. We should be able to understand their
need because we, too, want to know that we are of value to other
people. One of the ways we know we're needed is when others
express appreciation for *who we are* and *what we do.*

The Scriptures remind us that our major relationships involve
praise:

1. Praising God (see Psalm 100:4).
2. Praising our wives (see Proverbs 31:28).
3. Praising others; for example, our Christian friends (see
   Ephesians 4:29).

I can vividly remember my boss saying years ago, "If only I
had ten men like you, we could change the world." After that, I
was so motivated I couldn't do enough for him.

Teachers know how praise motivates children. One teacher
said she praised each student in her third-grade class every day,
without exception. Her students were the most motivated, encouraged, and enthusiastic in the school. When my substitute high
school geometry teacher praised me regularly, my D average
climbed to an A in six weeks.

Knowing how significant praise can be, why do we as husbands fail to express it to our wives? Several reasons. The most
common is preoccupation with our own needs, vocation, and
activities. We lose sight of the positive and helpful qualities in our

wives when we are preoccupied. Even worse, we fail to acknowledge our wives' helpful traits when we do notice them.

When a husband forgets his wife's need for praise, the marriage is usually on its way downhill. And if he constantly expresses the bitter instead of the sweet, his marriage will become less fulfilling every day. Criticism is devastating, especially when voiced in anger or harshness (see Proverbs 15:1, 4). When a husband rails against his wife for her unique feminine qualities, he conveys a lack of approval for her as a person. This automatically weakens their relationship.

Charlie Jones, in the book *Life Is Tremendous,* says we really can't enjoy life until we learn how to see and say something positive about everything. Though *none of us will ever be completely positive* about life, he says, we can be *in the process* of learning, growing, and developing toward a positive attitude.

If you develop a positive attitude, not only will others want to be around you more often, but your wife will also benefit tremendously. She will have a greater sense of worth and value, knowing you have provided the encouragement only a husband can give.

Encourage your wife and deepen your marriage relationship by following these two simple steps in learning how to praise her.

PRAISE HER (AT LEAST) ONCE A DAY

Promise yourself to tell your wife daily what you appreciate about her. Promise yourself—not her—because she might develop expectations and be hurt if you forget. Begin by learning to verbalize your thoughts of appreciation.

Here are some typical statements wives have told me they enjoy hearing:

1. "What a meal! The way you topped that casserole with sour cream and cheese . . . M-m-m-m . . . that was delicious."

2. (This next one is great with an early-morning kiss.) "Honey, I sure love you. You're special to me."

3. While in the company of friends say, "This is my wife. She's the greatest!"

4. Put little notes on the refrigerator like, "I loved the way you looked last night."

5. "You're such a dedicated wife to make my lunch every day."

6. "Our kids are really blessed to have a mother like you. You take such good care of them."

7. "I don't know if I prefer the dress or what's in it better."

8. "Do I like your hairstyle? I'd like any hairstyle you have just because it's on you."

9. "I'd love to take you out tonight just to show you off."

10. "Honey, you've worked so hard. Why don't you sit down and rest for a while before dinner? I can wait."

11. "You're so special to me that I'd like to do something special for you right now. Why don't you take a bubble bath and relax. I'll do up the dishes and get the kids started on their homework."

In her book *Forever My Love,* Margaret Hardisty emphasized that women tend to approach life on an emotional plane while men approach it on a more logical, sometimes coldly objective one. Therefore, when you praise your wife, it's important to use words and actions that communicate praise from *her point of view.* Anything that is romantic or deals with building deeper relationships usually pleases wives.

BE CREATIVE WITH YOUR PRAISE

One husband won his wife back partly through creative praise. He bought 365 pieces of wrapped candy, wrote a special message on every wrapper, and then sealed them again. She opened one piece every day and read what he appreciated about her for a full year.

A woman loves to find hidden notes—in her jewelry box, the silver drawer, the medicine cabinet. Search for ways to praise your wife. The possibilities are endless.

What kind of praise would you like to hear from your boss? Try a little of it on your wife. You may say, "Well, I don't need too much praise. I'm secure in my job, and I really don't need it." Then interview some of those who work with you to see how they would appreciate being praised. Some of their ideas might work with your wife. Also, ask your wife what kind of praise she likes to hear.

DON'T DRAW ATTENTION TO HER UNATTRACTIVE FEATURES

Wrinkles, gray hair, and excess weight are definitely not on the list of possible conversation starters. Even your casual comments about them can make your wife insecure—she may fear being traded in on a "newer model." She knows divorce is just too easy and common nowadays.

One husband wrote his wife a cute poem about how much he loved her little wrinkles and how he loved caressing her "cellulite." His card, though softened with flowers, made her cry for hours. Men, we have to praise our wives without drawing attention to what they believe are their unattractive features.

That doesn't mean you should use insincere flattery. Have you ever been to a party where someone compliments you, and you know inside the person doesn't mean what he or she says? Sometimes a husband will casually remark, "Oh, yeah, I really like that dress." But his wife can generally detect his insincerity. Even if you don't like her dress, you can say something sincere like, "Honey, the dress isn't half as good-looking as you are."

Did you know you can even find something to praise in your wife's faults? The chart "How to Find the Positive Side of Your Wife's 'Negative' Traits" can get you started on finding the positive aspects in the things you consider her "flaws."

HOW TO FIND THE POSITIVE SIDE OF YOUR WIFE'S "NEGATIVE" TRAITS

Negative	Positive
Nosy	She may be very *alert* or *sociable*.
Touchy	She may be very *sensitive*.
Manipulating	She may be a very *resourceful* person with many creative ideas.
Stingy	She may be very *thrifty*.
Talkative	She may be very *expressive* and *dramatic*.
Flighty	She may be an *enthusiastic* person with cheerful vitality.
Too serious	She may be a very *sincere* and *earnest* person with *strong convictions*.
Too bold	She may have *strong convictions*, *uncompromising* with her own standards.
Rigid	She may be a *well-disciplined* person with *strong convictions*.
Overbearing	She may be a very *confident* person—sure of herself.
A dreamer	She may be very *creative* and *imaginative*.
Too fussy	She may be very *organized* and *efficient*.

Specific praise is far better than *general* praise. For example, "That was a great dinner" doesn't do nearly as much for her as, "The asparagus with the nutmeg sauce was fantastic. I've never had asparagus that tasted so good. I don't know how you can take plain, ordinary vegetables and turn them into such mouthwatering delights."

"You're a great mom" won't send her into orbit, but this might: "I'm really grateful that I married a woman who is so sensitive that she knows just the perfect way of making our kids feel important. They're sure lucky to have such a sensitive mother."

There is no right or wrong time to praise your wife. She'll love it when you're alone or when you're with the children and friends. Make sure you don't limit your praise to public or private times. If you only praise her in public, she might suspect you're showing off for your friends. If you only praise her in private, she may feel you're embarrassed about doing it.

Whenever you praise her, it's important that your full attention be on her. If she senses that your mind or feelings are elsewhere, your praise will be less meaningful to her.

As you learn how to praise your wife genuinely and consistently, you'll begin to see a new sparkle in her eyes and new life in your relationship.

HOW TO TALK ABOUT PRAISE WITH YOUR WIFE

1. Learn to "Prime the Pump."

Husband: What kind of praise do you really enjoy receiving from people?

Wife: Oh, I don't know. As long as it's sincere, I'll like it.

Husband: Do you feel I praise you enough?

Wife: I think so.

Husband: (*priming the pump*) How about last week's meals? Would you appreciate it if I let you know more often how much I enjoy your cooking?

Wife: Oh, yes, I remember I went to a lot of extra effort on two meals last week, and you didn't even mention it. . . .

Now you've got the water flowing. If you can take it, keep pumping. Show your *concern* and *understanding* by saying things like, "That must really hurt you when I don't say anything. You deserve a medal for putting up with me." Comfort her and let her get rid of some of her pent-up feelings.

2. Look for the Hidden Meaning Behind Her Words.

Husband: Dear, remember last week when I thanked you for the meal? Did I overdo it in front of Steve and Mary?

Wife: Don't worry about it—it's okay.

Husband: Even when I said, "I'm glad we had company over; she's never cooked better"?

Wife: Oh, yeah, I did feel bad. You made it sound like I don't cook good meals for you unless we have company.

Husband: I thought you might have felt bad. Let's see, what would have been a better way to say what I meant?

A husband needs to help his wife be as honest and straightforward as possible so he can know where the relationship is strained. So many times during our early married years I asked Norma not to "beat around the bush" or "play games with me." I needed the facts in order to adjust my behavior and learn how to be a better husband. I hope you encourage your wife to be as straightforward as possible to help build a deeper, more fulfilling relationship.

Chapter Twelve

ARE YOU SOUL MATES?*
Dr. Les Parrott and Dr. Leslie Parrott

We are exactly alike," John blurted out. He and Nancy were one of a dozen newly married couples we were teaching. I (Leslie) had just asked each of them to talk about their differences when John made his proud exclamation. The other couples looked dismayed.

Les, as any psychologist would do, said, "Tell us about that, John."

Nancy nodded as her new husband replied, "We just don't have any big differences, that's all. We like all the same things and never disagree."

"Wow," Les said with a tinge of sarcasm in his voice. I felt myself starting to cringe, knowing what Les was thinking and hoping he wouldn't say it. But he did: "You are the first couple I have ever met that is exactly the same."

The class giggled, and John rolled his eyes. "Well, we are not *exactly* the same," he admitted.

Some couples strain to duplicate each other in order to cover up their differences. Newlyweds, for example, often force an unrealistic similarity upon their tastes, opinions, priorities, and habits. They do so with the best of intentions, but their sameness is no more real than Adam and Eve's when they covered their differences with fig leaves. God created each person to be different, and to deny that uniqueness leads only to pretense, not to partnership.

---

*Adapted from *Saving Your Marriage Before It Starts* by Dr. Les Parrott III and Dr. Leslie Parrott. Copyright © 1995 by Les and Leslie Parrott. Used by permission.

Another member of the same small group said, "Sharon and I have a fifty-fifty marriage, half and half." Other couples agreed. Sharing the load, even-steven, is a much better way to create oneness. "Yeah," said Sharon, "but sometimes our halves don't always fit together."

She's right. A "fifty-fifty marriage" only works if each partner is a fraction. But we aren't. Each of us is a whole person. We don't subtract something from ourselves when we get married. We remain whole, and we want to be loved as a whole, not cut to fit together.

We have seen couples try to build a marriage on the fifty-fifty principle, taking turns deciding this and that, splitting resources, weighing portions, counting privileges. But we have yet to find a fifty-fifty couple who doesn't feel that taking turns is cheating them out of their presumed rights. Often the more strong-willed partner, consciously or unconsciously, wields the knife that divides the "halves," and one half becomes "more equal" than the other.

So how then do a man and a woman become one in marriage? To put it another way: How do a man and a woman become soul mates? The answer is found exactly where you might suspect—deep in the soul. Recently, scientific research has backed up what common sense has been telling us for years; mainly, that tending to the spiritual dimension of marriage is what unites couples in unbreakable bonds.[1] Marriage thrives when its soul is nourished.

In this chapter we explore the most important and least talked about aspect of a healthy marriage—the spiritual dimension. We begin by exploring the need for spiritual intimacy and its deep meaning to your marriage. Next we show how God is revealed in your partnership and how marriage is closer to the nature of God than any other aspect of life. Then we outline some specific and practical tools for tending to the soul of your marriage. We conclude this chapter with a final remembrance.

SPIRITUAL INTIMACY: THE ULTIMATE MEANING OF MARRIAGE

On February 12, 1944, thirteen-year-old Anne Frank wrote the following words in her now-famous diary:

> Today the sun is shining, the sky is a deep blue, there is a lovely breeze and I am longing—so longing for everything. To talk, for freedom, for friends, to be alone.
>
> And I do so long . . . to cry! I feel as if I am going to burst, and I know that it would get better with crying, but I can't, I'm restless, I go from room to room, breathe through the crack of a closed window, feel my heart beating, as if it is saying, can't you satisfy my longing at last?
>
> I believe that it is spring within me, I feel that spring is awakening, I feel it in my whole body and soul. It is an effort to behave normally. I feel utterly confused. I don't know what to read, what to write, what to do, I only know that I am longing.

There is in all of us, at the very center of our lives, a tension, an aching, a burning in the heart that is deep and insatiable. Most often it is a longing without a clear name or focus, an aching that cannot be clearly pinpointed or described. Like Anne Frank, we only know that we are restless, aching deep within our soul.

Most people expect marriage to quench their soulful longing, and it often does for a time. But for many, the deep, restless aching echoes again. It certainly did for Roy and Pauline. They did everything they could to stack the odds for a strong marriage in their favor. They went through premarital counseling, adjusted faulty expectations, learned how to communicate effectively, practiced conflict resolution, and so on. They read books about marriage, attended seminars, listened to tapes, and even had an older couple who agreed to mentor them during their first married year. Roy and Pauline took marriage seriously, and their efforts were paying off—at least for the time being. They were now in their tenth year of marriage and, from all appearances, doing well. But in spite of all their effort, something was missing.

"We are very much in love," Pauline told us, "but sometimes it feels like we are just going through the motions."

"Yeah," said Roy. "We are definitely in love, but sometimes the relationship feels—I don't know—empty, I guess. Like there should be a deeper connection."

Roy and Pauline, in many respects, were a model couple. They did all the things healthy couples do. They were psychologically astute, emotionally balanced, and kept their relationship in working order. But their hearts continued to be restless, longing for something more, something deeper. Roy and Pauline, knowingly or not, were yearning to be soul mates.

What Roy and Pauline still needed to learn was that there is more to a thriving marriage than good communication, conflict resolution, and positive attitudes. While each of these tools is critically important for a lasting and meaningful relationship, they are not sufficient. Marriage is not a machine that needs routine maintenance to keep it functioning but a supernatural event founded upon a mutual exchange of holy pledges. Above all, marriage is a deep, mysterious, and unfathomable endeavor.

Even happily married couples like Roy and Pauline eventually discover an innate longing to bond with their lover, not just for comfort, not just for passion—but also for *meaning*. Our lives go on day after day. They may be successful or unsuccessful, full of pleasure or full of worry. But do they *mean* anything? Only our soul can answer.

For married couples, spiritual meaning should be a shared pursuit.[2] While every individual must come to an understanding of life's meaning alone, couples must also discover the meaning of their marriage together. You are not just husband and wife. You have given birth to a marriage that is very much like a living being, born from you both. And the soul of your new marriage needs nourishment.

Sharing life's ultimate meaning with another person is the spiritual call of soul mates, and every couple must answer that call or risk a stunted, underdeveloped marriage. Like yeast in a loaf of bread, spirituality will ultimately determine whether your marriage rises successfully or falls disappointingly flat.

The spiritual dimension of marriage is a practical source of food for marital growth and health. No single factor does more to cultivate oneness and a meaningful sense of purpose in marriage than a shared commitment to spiritual discovery. It is the ultimate hunger of our souls.

FINDING GOD IN YOUR MARRIAGE

One of the most compelling love stories in our time involves a couple who, in the beginning, lived an ocean apart. He was a scruffy old Oxford bachelor, a Christian apologist, and an author of best-selling books for children. She, an American, was much younger and divorced with two sons.

After first meeting during her visit to England in 1952, C. S. Lewis and Joy Davidson fed their relationship by mail. Intellectual sparks from the minds of each ignited their appreciation and respect for each other. When Joy moved to England with her boys, the relationship enjoyed the benefits of proximity. And when her departure from England seemed imminent because of a lack of funds and an expiring visitor's visa, C. S. Lewis made a decision: If Joy would agree, they would be married.

Early in the marriage, Joy's body revealed a secret it had kept hidden. She had cancer—and it was irreversible. The well-ordered life of C. S. Lewis suffered a meltdown. But in the process, the English man of letters realized how deep his love for Joy really was.

Moving on with their lives, the Lewises sought and got the added blessing of the church on their marriage, which had originally been formalized in a register's office. They gave Joy the best treatment available. Then he brought her home, committed to her care. It is not surprising that Joy's body responded. However, her remission was short-lived.

Near death, Joy told him, "You have made me happy." Then, a little while after, "I am at peace with God." Joy died at 10:15 that evening in 1960. "She smiled," Lewis later recalled, "but not at me."

If there is a lesson to be gained from this amazing love story, it must be that partners without a spiritual depth of oneness can never compete with the fullness of love that soul mates enjoy.

Marriage, when it is healthy, has a mystical way of revealing God; a way of bringing a smiling peace to our restless hearts.

When researchers examined the characteristics of happy couples who had been married for more than two decades, one of the most important qualities they found was "faith in God and spiritual commitment."[3] Religion, it has been proved, provides couples with a shared sense of values, ideology, and purpose that bolsters their partnership.

Marriage is closer to the nature of God than any other human experience. God uses the metaphor of marriage to describe relating to humanity: "As a bridegroom rejoices over his bride, so will your God rejoice over you."[4] God loves the church, "the bride," says Paul, not as a group of people external to himself with whom he has entered into an agreement, but as his own body.[5] And similarly, when a husband loves his wife and a wife her husband, as extensions of themselves, they live as "one flesh"—as soul mates.

Finally, through marriage, God also shows himself in two important ways: first, by revealing his faithfulness, and second, by revealing his forgiveness.

Marriage Reveals God's Faithfulness

What would marriage be like without faithfulness? What if the best we could ever get from our partner was "I'll try to be true, but don't count on it"? Of course, marriage would never survive. We would go insane with uncertainty if we could not count on our mate's faithfulness. The livelihood of our relationship depends on the strength of faithfulness—theirs, ours, and ultimately God's.

Yes, God's faithfulness is essential to the survival of our marriages. Think about it. How can we, weak and limited persons that we are, look all the uncertainty of life full in the face and say, "I will make one thing certain: my faithfulness to my partner"? We can't, at least not on our own.

Robertson McQuilkin is a husband who is known for relying on God's faithfulness. He was a Christian college president and his wife, Muriel, was the host of a successful radio program when Muriel began to experience memory failure. The medical diagnosis turned their forty-two-year marriage inside out: Muriel had Alzheimer's.

"It did not seem painful to her," said Robertson, "but it was a slow dying for me to watch the creative, articulate person I knew and loved gradually dimming out." Robertson approached his college board of trustees and asked them to begin the search for his successor, telling them that when the day came that Muriel needed him full-time, she would have him.

Because Robertson still had eight years to go before retirement, his friends urged him to arrange for the institutionalization of Muriel. She will become accustomed to her new environment quickly, they said. *But would she?* Robertson asked himself. *Would anyone love her at all, let alone love her as I do?* Eventually Muriel could not speak in sentences, only words, and often words that made little sense. But she could say one sentence, and she said it often: "I love you."

The college board arranged for a companion to stay with Muriel so Dr. McQuilkin could go daily to his office. During that time it became increasingly difficult to keep Muriel home. When Robertson left, she would take out after him. The walk to the college was a mile roundtrip from their house, and Muriel would make the trip as many as ten times a day. "Sometimes at night," said Robertson, "when I helped her undress, I found bloody feet. When I told our family doctor, he choked up and simply said, 'Such love.'"

In 1990, believing that being faithful to Muriel "in sickness and in health" was a matter of integrity, Robertson McQuilkin resigned his presidency to care for his wife full-time. "Daily, I discern new manifestations of the kind of person she is," he has said. "I also see fresh manifestations of God's love—the God I long to love more fully."

Several years have passed since Robertson's resignation, and Muriel has steadily declined so that now she rarely speaks. She sits most of the time while he writes, yet she is contented and often bubbles with laughter. "She seems still to have affection for me," says Robertson. "What more could I ask? I have a home full of love and laughter; many couples with their wits about them don't have that! Muriel is very lovable—more dear to me now than ever. When she reaches out to me in the night hours or smiles contentedly and lovingly as she awakes, I thank the Lord for his grace to us and ask him to let me keep her."

Faithfulness is like a multifaceted jewel, exhibiting a complex combination of interrelated dimensions—trust, commitment, truth, loyalty, valuing, care. But our faithfulness to each other can only be sustained by God's model of faithfulness to us. When a man and woman covenant with one another, God promises faithfulness to them. And that helps couples keep the faith.

There is no way to overemphasize the centrality of faithfulness in God's character. It is woven into every part of the Bible—from Genesis, where God initiates his promise of faithfulness, through Revelation, where John's vision depicts "a white horse, whose rider is called Faithful and True."[6] Great is God's faithfulness. Even when we are faithless, God will remain faithful, "for he cannot disown himself."[7]

God's covenantal faithfulness, embodied in our partner, makes a home for our restless hearts. It accepts our whole soul by saying, "I believe in you and commit myself to you through thick and thin." Without faithfulness and the trust it engenders, marriage would have no hope of enduring. For no couple can achieve deep confidence in the fidelity of themselves and each other until they first recognize God's faithfulness to them.

Marriage Reveals God's Forgiveness

While we were living in Los Angeles, a friend invited us to tour the Hollywood film studio where she worked. We rode across the lot on a handy golf cart and quietly ducked into soundstages to catch behind-the-scene glimpses of familiar faces. One of the highlights was watching the filming of an episode of the hit TV show *Thirtysomething*. Our friend, observing our interest in this particular show, later sent us an autographed script. It featured Nancy and Elliot, a struggling married couple, in a brutal counseling session. Finally Elliot says, "I don't know if I love Nancy anymore. . . . And no matter what she does, I can't seem to forgive her for that."

Forgiveness lies at the heart of marriage. Two people living together, day after day, stumbling over each other's beings, are bound to cause pain, sometimes innocently, sometimes not. And if forgiveness is not given to cleanse the marriage soul, condemnation hovers over the relationship. Resentment piles on top of resentment until we blame our partners, not just for their wrongdoing, but for our failure to forgive them too.

This is a red-light danger zone. Human forgiveness was never designed to be given on a grand scale. Forgiveness in marriage can only heal when the focus is on what our spouses do, not on who they are. Partners forgive best for specific acts. Trying to forgive carte blanche is silly. Nobody can do it but God.

We overload the circuits of forgiveness when we try to forgive our partner for not being the sort of partner we want him or her to be. There are other means for coping with this: courage, empathy, patience, hope. But for mere human beings, forgiveness in the grand manner must be left to God. For it is God's forgiveness that empowers our ability to forgive the relatively small things—no minor miracle in itself. Every couple needs to forgive. I (Leslie) had a hard time accepting that. Why would I ever need to forgive Les, the man who had pledged his love to me unto death? Somehow I thought that if forgiveness was necessary, our relationship was failing. I was too proud to admit that Les could hurt me. But at times he did. And of course, I hurt him. In fact, I have learned that most of the time, forgiveness in marriage is usually not about an innocent lamb and a bad wolf. Most of the time I have to do my forgiving while being forgiven—by God, if not by my husband.

When we forgive a partner, we are revealing God's love to him or her, free from condemnation. Human forgiveness enlightens divine forgiveness.

Loving your partner as yourself is probably the single most wholehearted step you will ever take to fulfill the love of God. Such a step, of course, could never even be contemplated without the enabling grace of God. While many marriages are undertaken—and even manage to last—without a conscious reliance on God's help, there are no meaningful partnerships without the continuing secret touch of God's grace on the soul of their marriage.

TENDING THE SOUL OF YOUR MARRIAGE

Superficiality is the curse of a restless marriage. The desperate need of most marriages is not for more excitement, more glitz, more activity. The soul of your marriage yearns for depth.

At least three classic disciplines of the spiritual life call soul mates to move beyond surface living and into the depths: worship, service, and prayer. In the midst of our normal daily activities, these disciplines have a transforming power to quiet the spirit and nurture our marriage.[8] By the way, these disciplines are not for spiritual giants, nor are they some dull drudgery designed to extinguish all the fun in your life. The only requirement to practice these disciplines is a longing for God to fill your marriage.

Worship

We have a Norman Rockwell print that depicts a family on Sunday morning. The husband, unshaven, messy-haired, and ensconced in pajamas and bathrobe, is slumped in a chair with portions of the Sunday paper strewn about. Behind him is his wife, dressed in a tailored suit and on her way to church. The picture is a playful reminder to us of how important shared worship is to the soul of our marriage.

Both of us grew up going to church. It was a part of our heritage. As surely as the sun came up in the east, our families would be in church on Sunday morning. Going to church wasn't questioned. It was just something you did. Case closed.

But when we got married and moved far from home, worship was suddenly an option. In a new city, we were faced with the opportunity of establishing our own routines, our own weekly patterns. For the first time, going to church was something we were not compelled to do. Nobody was going to call and ask where we were. Nobody was checking up on us. We could now stay home on Sundays, take a hike, sit in the sun, read a book. Or we could go to church. We did.

From the beginning of our marriage, shared worship has been a systematic time of rest and renewal for our relationship. Dedicating a day of the week to worship stabilizes our marriage and liberates us from the tyranny of productivity that fills our other days. The church where we worship is a place of social support and spiritual refueling. Singing hymns, learning from Scripture, worshiping God, and meeting with friends who share our spiritual quest is comforting and inspiring. Worshiping together buoys our relationship and makes the week ahead more meaningful.

And once again, research supports our decision to worship together as a means of nurturing the soul of our marriage. A recent study showed that couples who attended church together even as little as once a month increase their chances of staying married for life. Studies have also shown that churchgoers feel better about their marriages than those who don't worship together![9]

Worship has a way of transforming relationships. To stand before the Holy One of eternity is to grow and change. In worship, God's transforming power steals its way into the sanctuary of our hearts and enlarges our capacity to love.

Service

"I never knew how selfish I was until I got married," said Gary. After six months of marriage, he was telling us how Paula, his wife, was volunteering at a retirement center one night a week. "At first I resented her being away from me. But a couple of months ago she needed a lift, so I went with her." He came back with Paula again and again, until he discovered that helping the older people at the center had become the highlight of his week. "It feels good to help others, and it brings Paula and me closer together; it's like we are a team that is making a difference," he told us.

We have heard dozens of similar reports from couples. There is something good about reaching out as a team. Almost mystically it becomes bonding. Reaching out to others promotes humility, sharing, compassion, and intimacy in a marriage. Doing good for others helps couples transcend themselves and become part of something larger.[10]

There are literally hundreds of ways to incorporate shared service into your marriage. The key is to find some thing that fits your personal style. For example, we have two couples in our neighborhood who both actively practice reaching out, but in different ways. Steve and Thanne Moore live in the house across the street from us and have been married fifteen years. They sponsor a needy child, Robert Jacques, who lives in Haiti. Every month they send him cards and letters as well as money to provide education, clothes, and food. On special occasions, Steve and Thanne will have their three children draw pictures to send to Robert. Twice, Steve and Thanne have even traveled to Haiti to be with Robert at his orphanage. Someday, they hope to see him in college.

Two blocks down the street in our neighborhood live Dennis and Lucy Guernsey. They have been married twenty-five years, and from the beginning they made a joint decision: to have an open home and be generous with others. Everyone who knows Dennis and Lucy knows of their hospitality. They have made their home a hub of celebration and delicious dinners. Sometimes it's casual and spontaneous, sometimes planned and elegant, but always, it is special. They throw graduation parties, birthday parties, welcome-to-the-neighborhood parties. They have showers and receptions. And on Mother's Day they invite single moms for Sunday brunch.

If you ask either Dennis and Lucy or Steve and Thanne why they reach out the way they do, they will tell you how fulfilling it is to make others happy. But they will also tell you about the deep bond their shared service brings to their own marriage.

We know lots of couples who can testify to how meaningful reaching out to others is to their marriage. Whether it be sponsoring a needy child, opening your home to guests, giving blankets to the homeless, or baking cookies for prisoners, doing good for others is good for marriage. For soul mates, true service is not self-righteous, it's not done for rewards, it's not a "big deal." It comes from whispered promptings, divine urgings deep within the soul of your marriage.

One more thing about serving together. If all of your service is before others, it will remain shallow. Service is sometimes done in secret, concealed from everyone but the two of you. We find that the soul of our marriage is satisfied most when we do something, even small things, anonymously. To secretly observe the results of our service brings deeper devotion and intimacy.

Tending the soul of your marriage requires constant attention. For if you neglect the soul of your marriage there will be only superficial bonding, which rides the waves of *emotion and infatuation* until the marriage is beached. But if in your sojourn together you tend the soul—through worship, service, and prayer—you will make it through the storms of marriage unscathed.

Prayer

Sociologist Andrew Greeley surveyed married people and found that the happiest couples were those who pray together. Couples who frequently pray together are twice as likely as those who pray less often to describe their marriages as being highly romantic. They also report considerably higher sexual satisfaction and more sexual ecstasy!

There is an old story about a young couple who decided to start their honeymoon by kneeling beside their bed to pray. The bride giggled when she heard her new husband's prayer: "For what we are about to receive may the Lord make us truly thankful."

As strange as it may sound, there is a strong link in marriage between prayer and sex. For one thing, frequency of prayer is a more powerful predictor of marital satisfaction than frequency of sexual intimacy. But get this: Married couples who pray together are ninety percent more likely to report higher satisfaction with their sex life than couples who do not pray together. Also, women who pray with their partner tend to be more orgasmic. That doesn't sound right, does it? After all, married churchgoers are painted by the media as prudes who think sex is dirty. Well, let the media say what they want, but prayerful couples know better.

Few couples have come into our office more devout than Tom and Kathleen. They attended church regularly. Kathleen sang in the choir; Tom taught junior high Sunday school. Kathleen was in a women's Bible study; Tom was in a men's accountability group. Everyone in their church looked to Tom and Kathleen as dedicated and vibrant spiritual leaders. But when the two of them came to see us, their five-year-old marriage was falling apart at the seams. They told us their story, one we had heard many times. They were overinvolved with everything but their marriage and as a result had "fallen out of love." In spite of all their spiritual fervor, Tom and Kathleen had allowed the soul of their marriage to wither.

"When was the last time the two of you prayed together?" one of us asked. Tom and Kathleen looked at each other, and the answer was obvious: It had been a long, long time.

We talked with Tom and Kathleen a bit longer and gave them a simple assignment, an experiment really. For the next week they were to pray briefly together just before going to bed.

Five days later we received a call: "This is Kathleen. I know this sounds crazy, but our relationship has done an about-face." She told us how spending a moment together in prayer was rejuvenating their spirits and their marriage.

No amount of being "religious" can make up for the time couples spend in shared prayer. But if prayer is so good for a marriage, you may be asking, why don't more couples do it? Because it's not easy. Praying is vulnerable, and anytime we let our guard down, even with our spouse, it can be threatening (this is especially true for men). After all, our partner knows firsthand what we are really like. He or she sees us when nobody else is watching. So how can I be completely candid before God with my partner listening in? How can I express my true hopes and fears, my pain, the sins that grip me? No wonder many couples opt out of prayer. The price of its vulnerability seems too high.

Praying together as a couple, we must confess, has not always been natural or easy for Leslie and me. We have at times both fallen into the trap of preaching through our prayers and subtly jabbing each other with our "good" intentions. But through the years we have picked up some principles that have helped us pray more effectively. First, we pray a prayer of thanksgiving. That's all. Rather than trying to pray about our needs or difficulties, we simply give thanks to God. Occasionally we say the Lord's Prayer together (see Matthew 6:9–13). And sometimes one of us will simply initiate a time of silent prayer together or a time of listening to God or maybe a time of brief sentence prayers. The point is to pray. There is no right or wrong way to do it. Every attempt we make to commune with God in shared prayer nurtures the soul of marriage.

SO REMEMBER THIS

Like most couples deeply in love, we longed to be soul mates even before we were married. Part of the impetus for our vision came from reading *A Severe Mercy,* the real-life love story about Sheldon and Davy Vanauken, two lovers who not only dreamed about building a soulful union but devised a concrete strategy for doing so called their Shining Barrier. Its goal: to make their love invulnerable. Its plan: to share *everything.* Everything! If one of them liked something, they decided, there must be something to like in it—and the other must find it. Whether it be poetry, strawberries, or an interest in ships, Sheldon and Davy committed to share every single thing either of them liked. That way they would create a thousand strands, great and small, that would link them together. They reasoned that by sharing everything they would become so close that it would be impossible, unthinkable, for either of them to suppose that they could ever recreate such closeness with anyone else. Total sharing, they felt, was the ultimate secret of a love that would last forever.

To be the watch upon the walls of the Shining Barrier, Sheldon and Davy established what they called the Navigators' Council. It was an inquiry into the state of their union. Were they fully sharing? Was there any sign of growing apart? More than once a month they would intentionally talk about their relationship and evaluate their activities by asking: Is this best for our love?

Something about this Shining Barrier—a shield to protect one's love and build a fortified bond—appealed to Leslie and me. We wanted to guard against losing the glory of love. We did not fear divorce as much as we feared a more subtle enemy—gradual separateness. Looking about us, we saw marriages perishing because the couples took love for granted. Ceasing to do things together, finding separate interests, couples we knew were turning "we" into "I" as their marriages aged. We observed a subtle separateness creeping into their marriage with barely a notice—each of them going off to their separate jobs in separate worlds while their apartness was quietly tearing at their union. Why let this happen to us? Why not raise the Shining Barrier as Sheldon and Davy did?

We were inspired.

Late in the spring, just days before our wedding, we sat on a bench talking about our love and impending commitment and concluded that there was something cold about making a contractual agreement, a binding commitment, to stay together. We didn't want to perform marital "duties" because we *had* to, because we were locked into it externally. We were looking for a deeper bond that transcended even the idealized vestiges of the Shining Barrier. That's when the real lesson of Sheldon and Davy's story hit us: that becoming soul mates ultimately requires more than an appeal to love, more than a commitment to extravagant sharing. It requires an appeal to God.

The aching, burning urge you and your partner have to be connected—soul to soul—can only be quenched when your spirits are joined by a greater Spirit, Jesus Christ—the ultimate Shining Barrier. So remember this: The sacred secret to becoming soul mates is pursuing a mutual communion with God.

NOTES

CHAPTER 2: GET TOUGH!

1. Jeanette Lauer and Robert Lauer, "Marriages Made to Last," *Psychology Today,* June 1985, 22–26.

2. Robert J. Sternberg, "A Triangular Theory of Love," *Psychological Review* 93, no. 2 (1986): 119–35 (quote is from p. 123).

3. See my book *Make Anger Your Ally,* 3d ed. (Colorado Springs: Focus on the Family, 1990).

CHAPTER 4: MEMO TO MOM AND DAD: THE KIDS AND THE JOB DON'T COME FIRST!

1. Charles Hummel, *The Tyranny of the Urgent* (Downers Grove, Ill.: InterVarsity Press, 1971), 4.

2. Dr. Kevin Leman, *Bonkers: Why Women Get Stressed Out and What They Can Do About It* (New York: Dell, 1990).

3. Mary Ellen Schoonmaker, "The New Decade: What's in Your Future?" *Family Circle,* 9 January 1990, 42.

4. Sarah Rimer, "Sequencers: Putting Careers on Hold," *New York Times,* 23 September 1988, A21.

5. Felice Schwartz, "Management Women and the New Facts of Life," *Harvard Business Review,* January/February 1989, 65.

6. Paul J. Rosch, M.D., president, American Institute of Stress, in a letter to the *New York Times,* 12 December 1986.

7. Reality Discipline is a concept that has its roots in the work of psychiatrists such as Rudolph Dreikurs, but you can find the same basic idea in the biblical reminder that all of us "reap what we sow" (Galatians 6:7). It centers around letting life do the disciplining, letting us face the consequences of our own behavior. Reality Discipline centers on rules, agreements, or laws that are set up ahead of time with the understanding that if we fail to obey the rules, certain consequences will result. For more on Reality Discipline, see my book *Making Children Mind Without Losing Yours* (Dell, 1987).

8. Jim Schachter, "The Daddy Track," *Los Angeles Times Magazine,* 1 October 1989, 16.

9. Schachter, "The Daddy Track," 16.

CHAPTER 6: CHANGE IS POSSIBLE

1. Observing the long-term effects of living by this philosophy might eventually compel an honest publisher to retitle the work *Victim's Descent into Hell.* I suggest reading the episode in *Pilgrim's Progress* where Pilgrim meets Mr. Worldly Wiseman, who directs him to the town of Morality and to Mr. Legalist and his son Civility. A careful reading of this passage and of Evangelist's rebuke of Pilgrim for heeding Mr. Worldly Wiseman's counsel would be time well spent.

2. Godly living can be said to be natural to a Christian in that it is consistent with the desire to please God present in every regenerated heart.

3. "Natural Men in a Dreadful Conditon," *Select Works of Jonathan Edwards,* vol. 1, ed. Ian Murray (The Banner of Truth Trust, 1965).

CHAPTER 7: NEVER QUIT!

1. Michael McManus, *Marriage Savers: Helping Your Friends and Family Avoid Divorce* (Grand Rapids: Zondervan, 1995), 28.

2. Josh McDowell, *The Secret of Loving* (Wheaton, Ill.: Tyndale, 1987), 311.

CHAPTER 8: DO YOU KNOW HOW TO FIGHT A GOOD FIGHT?

1. H. J. Markman, "Constructive Marital Conflict Is Not an Oxymoron," *Behavioral Assessment* 13 (1991): 83–96.

2. H. J. Markman, S. Stanley, F. Floyd, K. Hahlweg, and S. Blumberg, "Prevention of Divorce and Marital Distress," *Psychotherapy Research* (1992).

3. E. Bader, "Do Marriage Preparation Programs Really Help?" (paper presented at the National Council on Family Relations Annual Conference, Milwaukee, Wisconsin, 1981).

4. E. L. Boroughs, "Love and Money," *U.S. News & World Report,* 19 October 1992, 54–60. G. Hudson, "Money Fights," *Parents,* February 1992, 75–79.

5. For more information about these four disastrous ways of interacting, see John Gottman's *Why Marriages Succeed or Fail* (New York: Simon & Schuster, 1994).

6. F. D. Cox, *Human Intimacy: Marriage, the Family, and Its Meaning* (New York: West, 1990).

7. C. Notarius and H. Markman, *We Can Work It Out: Making Sense of Marital Conflict* (New York: Putnam, 1993).

CHAPTER 9: THE UNION FIDELITY LOVE BANK IS ALWAYS OPEN

1. Willard F. Harley Jr., *His Needs, Her Needs* (Old Tappan, N.J.: Revell, 1986), chapter 2.

2. For a brief definition of Reality Discipline, see chapter 4, note 7.

3. Trish Hall, "Breaking Up Is Becoming Harder to Do," *New York Times,* 14 March 1991, C1.

4. Quoted in Victoria Sackett, "Couples Discovering Marriages Can Be Saved," *USA Today,* 2 April 1991, 13A.

5. Harley, *His Needs, Her Needs,* 70.

CHAPTER 10: NEGOTIATE A MUTUALLY SATISFYING SEXUAL RELATIONSHIP

1. Robert T. Michael, John H. Gagnon, Edward O. Laumann, and Gina Kolata, *Sex in America: A Definitive Survey* (Boston: Little, Brown and Company, 1994).

2. Clifford L. Penner and Joyce J. Penner, *The Gift of Sex* (Dallas: Word, 1981).

3. Clifford L. Penner and Joyce J. Penner, *Restoring the Pleasure* (Dallas: Word, 1994).

CHAPTER 12: ARE YOU SOUL MATES?

1. E. E. Lauer, "The Holiness of Marriage: Some New Perspectives from a Recent Sacramental Theology," *The Journal of Ongoing Formation* 6 (1985): 215–26.

2. D. R. Leckey, "The Spirituality of Marriage: A Pilgrimage of Sorts," *The Journal of Ongoing Formation* 6 (1985): 227–40.

3. D. L. Fenell, "Characteristics of Long-term First Marriages," *Journal of Mental Health Counseling* 15 (1993): 446–60.

4. Isaiah 62:5.

5. Not infrequently God is called "a jealous God" (see Exodus 20:5; 34:14; Deuteronomy 4:24; 5:9; 6:15). This phrase may sound strange to modern ears, but there is a beautiful idea behind it. The picture is that of God as the passionate lover of our souls. Love is always exclusive; no one can be totally in love with two people at the same time. To say that God is a jealous God is to say that God is the lover of men and women, and that his heart can brook no rival, but that he must have the whole devotion of our hearts. The divine-human relationship is not that of king and subject, nor that of master and servant, nor that of owner and slave, nor that of judge and defendant, but that of lover and loved one, a relationship that can only be paralleled in the perfect marriage relationship between husband and wife.

6. Revelation 19:11.

7. 2 Timothy 2:13.

8. L. M. Foerster, "Spiritual Practices and Marital Adjustment in Lay Church Members and Graduate Theology Students," Dissertation, Graduate School of Psychology, Fuller Theological Seminary, Pasadena, California, 1984.

9. S. T. Ortega, "Religious Homogamy and Marital Happiness," *Journal of Family Issues* 2 (1988): 224–39.

10. D. A. Abbott, M. Berry, and W. H. Meredith, "Religious Belief and Practice: A Potential Asset in Helping Families," *Family Relations* (1990): 443–48.

Women of Faith is partnering with Zondervan Publishing House, Integrity Music, *Today's Christian Woman* magazine, and Campus Crusade to offer conferences, publications, worship music, and inspirational gifts that support and encourage today's Christian women.

Since their beginning in January of 1996, the Women of Faith conferences have enjoyed an enthusiastic welcome by women across the country.

Call 1-888-49-FAITH for the many conference locations and dates available.

www.women-of-faith.com

See the following page for additional information about Women of Faith products.

Stop and Savor the Joy!

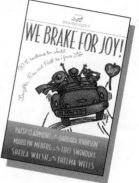

Finding Joy in the Journey

Joy Breaks

The original rest-stop devotional for women traveling the joyful journey. The warm and witty team of Clairmont, Johnson, Meberg, and Swindoll encourage women to lighten up, laugh, and cast their cares on the One whose yoke is easy and whose burden is light.

Hardcover, ISBN: 0-310-21345-2

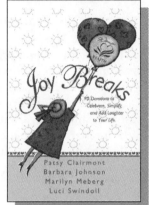

Joy Breaks Daybreak®

128-page perpetual calendar

ISBN: 0-310-97287-6

A Trustworthy Road Map
for Women of Faith

The Joyful Journey

Women of Faith conference speakers Patsy Clairmont, Barbara Johnson, Marilyn Meberg, and Luci Swindoll speak straight from their hearts about the obstacles, bumps, and detours we sometimes face along the journey of life and how to steer our hearts closer to God.

New! Softcover ISBN: 0-310-22155-2
Hardcover ISBN: 0-310-21344-4

The Joyful Journey Audio Pages

The authors read their favorite chapters.
Two 60-minute cassettes

ISBN: 0-310-21454-8

The Joyful Journey Daybreak®

366-day perpetual calendar

ISBN: 0-310-97282-5

Hitting You September '98!

Boomerang Joy

Best-selling author Barbara Johnson is known for her far-flung humor. Now she's flying at you with her first-ever devotional. In it, she'll teach readers how to "fling a smile a mile." But be ready, she warns: "It'll come right back to you, more accurately each time you toss it out."

Hardcover, **ISBN: 0-310-22006-8**

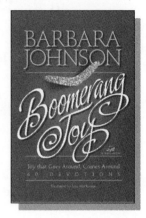

Boomerang Joy Audio Pages

Read by the uproariously funny author herself.
Two 60-minute cassettes
ISBN: 0-310-22548-5

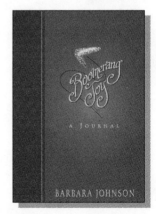

Boomerang Joy Journal

Includes NIV Scripture prompts. Two-color interior. 128 lined pages, 5" x 7 1/8"

ISBN: 0-310-97708-8

Reclaim the Joy!

Bring Back the Joy

Sheila Walsh illustrates the things that steal our joy and gives practical steps to restoring joy at a depth most of us have only imagined—through resting in the one who is Joy.

Hardcover, **ISBN: 0-310-22023-8**

Bring Back the Joy Audio Pages

Read by the author.
Two 60-minute cassettes

ISBN: 0-310-22222-2

A Celebration of Friendship

Friends Through Thick & Thin

Using the metaphor of a garden, close
friends Gloria Gaither, Peggy Benson,
Sue Buchanan, and Joy MacKenzie offer
insights into creating a life-enriching
circle of friends. Each short chapter is a
down-to-earth slice of life.

Hardcover, **ISBN: 0-310-21726-1**

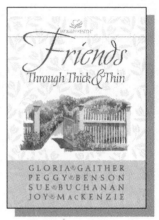

Bring Back the Joy!

NIV Spiritual Renewal Bible

Based on proven insights from Steve Arterburn's highly successful *Life Recovery Bible* (Tyndale), the *NIV Spiritual Renewal Bible* is designed to lead the parched traveler to springs of spiritual refreshment. Readers follow two seven-step reading plans (Old Testament and New Testament) and are encouraged to apply the spiritual disciplines of prayer, service, fasting, and meditation.

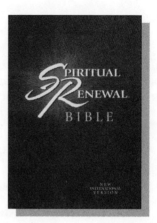

Hardcover ISBN: 0-310-91857-X
Softcover ISBN: 0-310-91858-8
Burgundy Bonded Leather ISBN: 0-310-91859-6

Wisdom, prayers, and promises...

Capturing the Joy

Prayers for a Woman of Faith

This latest title helps meet the needs of women who desire a deeper prayer life. Like the other two titles in this series, these inspiring NIV Scriptures are arranged topically.

ISBN: 0-310-97336-8

Promises of Joy for a Woman of Faith

ISBN: 0-310-97389-9

Words of Wisdom for a Woman of Faith

ISBN: 0-310-97390-2

Joy for a Woman's Soul

This personal-sized book promises to refresh
the spirit with its beautiful four-color images,
Scripture from the NIV Bible, and choice
quotes from best-selling Women of Faith
authors.

ISBN: 0-310-97717-7

Small Group Bible Studies...

for women who want to travel the Joyful Journey

Women of Faith Bible Study Series

At last! A Bible study series designed especially for women that helps link them together in bonds of friendship, joy, faith, and prayer. New from Women of Faith, this exciting small-group Bible study series helps women grow up in Christ and outward in fellowship as they share their spiritual journeys with one another.

Six lessons in each guide include quiet moments for reflection, discussion questions, friendship boosters, fun activities, and prayer. Leader's notes are included.

Experiencing God's Presence
0-310-21343-6

Knowing God's Will
0-310-21339-8

Strengthening Your Faith
0-310-21337-1

Growing in Prayer
0-310-21335-5

Embracing Forgiveness
0-310-21341-X

Discovering Your Spiritual Gifts
0-310-21340-1

Finding Joy
0-310-21336-3

Celebrating Friendship
0-310-21338-X

THE OFFICIAL NEW
WOMEN OF FAITH™
RECORDINGS
ONLY ON INTEGRITY MUSIC

We want to hear from you. Please send your comments about this
book to us in care of the address below. Thank you.

ZondervanPublishingHouse
Grand Rapids, Michigan 49530
http://www.zondervan.com